M000306008

DAILY MEDITATIONS
WITH
SAINT AUGUSTINE

DAILY MEDITATIONS
WITH
SAINT AUGUSTINE

MINUTE MEDITATIONS FOR EVERY DAY
TAKEN FROM THE WRITINGS
OF SAINT AUGUSTINE

Compiled and Edited
by
John E. Rotelle, O.S.A.

Illustrated

CATHOLIC BOOK PUBLISHING CO.
New Jersey

CONTENTS

NIHIL OBSTAT: Rev. James M. Cafone, M.A., S.T.D.
Censor Librorum

IMPRIMATUR: ✠ Most Rev. John J. Myers, D.D., J.C.D.
Archbishop of Newark

The Nihil Obstat and Imprimatur are official declarations that a book or a pamphlet is free of doctrinal or moral error. No implication is contained therein that those who have granted the Nihil Obstat and Imprimatur agree with the contents, opinions or statements expressed.

(T-176)

INTRODUCTION

ONE of the aims of every follower of Christ is to have the mind of a Christian. In this regard, we could do no better than to follow a man who had one of the greatest minds of all time as well as one of the most Christian of minds—St. Augustine of Hippo.

Indeed, Augustine fits our modern mentality better than any thinker of the past. That's because he thought with his heart as well as his head. He was ever-conscious of the weakness and sinfulness of humankind—never ruling out evil and always aware that human beings could go from the heights to the depths and vice versa in quick fashion.

Moreover, Augustine knew the power of love. Indeed, he regarded it as the most powerful force in the world. More than any other ancient writer, Augustine made the "law of love" stand out. He reduced the whole of moral theology to charity or love: "The purpose of every precept is charity, i.e., every precept is referred to love."

Augustine had the knack of forging compelling and memorable expressions. He honed his literary skills and used them to communicate the Christian thoughts of a razor-sharp mind. He was a wordsmith beyond compare!

Not only is Augustine's language crystal-clear, riveting, and ever-memorable. Its Christian content is sure and unerring. After his conversion Augustine was driven more than ever by his lifelong quest for God, a quest graphically illustrated by the following legendary story.

One day Augustine came upon a little boy engrossed in filling a cup with water from the ocean and running to pour it into a hole he had made in the sand. Time after time he repeated this action, prompting the Saint to ask: "What is that you're doing?" The boy said: "I'm going to put the whole ocean into this hole."

Augustine smiled and said: "Son, you can't do that. The ocean is too big for this little hole." The boy looked up with a smile and answered: "Neither can you fit all of God into your tiny brain." But Augustine never stopped trying.

Augustine forged five Christian maxims that can be used to sum up the Christian mind.

1. *"You have made us for Yourself O Lord, and our hearts are restless till they rest in You."*

Augustine eloquently taught that God is the true object of our human restlessness and insatiable quest for happiness. All human beings, in all that they do, seek God, and nothing else can satisfy their lifelong hunger for Him.

Augustine sought God in many avenues without success before realizing Who it was that he sought and receiving the grace to find Him.

Augustine's oft-repeated words are a constant reminder to all of us about what our real purpose in life is. They can help us stay on the right path amid the distractions of the world.

2. *"Love, and do what you will."*

As already mentioned, love is the most powerful force in the world. Those who truly love God will do nothing but what is pleasing to Him.

Indeed, it is well-nigh impossible for them to do what is displeasing to God. True love will find a way to do good!

Hence, it was natural for Augustine to create a phrase that can be called the ultimate Christian motto: "Love, and do what you will"—because in such a case your will is necessarily in tune with the will of your Beloved, Who is God!

3. *"For you I am a Bishop; with you I am a Christian."*

Augustine never subscribed to a laity-clergy dichotomy in his theology. His position as a Bishop was one of religious power, but he never forgot that he was as human as his people.

He was one of them—engaged on the journey to the Promised Land. Just because he was a Bishop did not mean he was above the Christian struggle. He did not lord it over his people.

These are words that every Christian pastor can say to reassure his people concerning his service to them and his solidarity with them. The same is true of all Christians in authority. They are words of consolation for everyone.

4. *"Seek not to understand that you may believe but seek to believe that you may understand."*

With these words Augustine reminds us of the supreme importance of faith in the Christian approach to life. In his view, Christian thinkers start from faith before understanding. They seek to understand—but only after believing! They then explain what they believe.

This is a particularly prized formula for Christians who "walk by faith and not by sight" and who practice "faith seeking understanding."

5. *"We are an Easter people and Alleluia is our song."*

Augustine appreciated the power of Christ's redeeming Passion and Resurrection. So, he never let his people forget their redeemed state.

Easter turned the whole world upside down for the better. It provided untold powers for human beings and opened up a future of eternal bliss for those who want to attain it.

All who dwell on this magnificent Christian destiny can only exclaim "Alleluia" ("Praise the Lord") and exult in being an Easter people!

This little book of minute meditations and prayers from the works of St. Augustine was put together by Father John Rotelle, a devoted follower of Christ and Augustine, although he did not live to see the final product. He intended it to be a companion volume to *Augustine Day by Day,* which we published in 1985.

May it serve to fashion more dedicated followers of Augustine and therefore of Christ, the Lord Whom both Father Rotelle and St. Augustine followed so closely in their lives on earth.

The Publishers

JANUARY 1
Mother of God

JESUS already was before He was made and, being almighty, He was able to be made while remaining what He was. He made a Mother for Himself while still with the Father and, when He was made from His Mother, He remained in the Father.

How could He cease to be God on beginning to be Man when He enabled His Mother not to cease to be a Virgin when she gave Him birth? —*Sermon 186, 1*

PRAYER. *You are the one, eternal, true substance, O God, in which there is perfect harmony, perfect charity, perfect life.*

—*Soliloquies I, 1, 3*

JANUARY 2
Be in Attendance at the Manger

THE inn was crowded so He was wrapped in rags, laid in a manger. The One Who filled the universe could find no room in a lodging house; laid in a feeding-trough, He became our food.

Let the two animals approach the manger, the two peoples. The ox, you see, recognizes its owner, and the donkey its master's manger. Be in attendance at the manger; don't be ashamed of being the Lord's donkey! —*Sermon 189, 4*

PRAYER. *I am not now asking for earthly goods, O God, for I have learned from Your new covenant what holier things to desire.*

—*On Ps. 137, 1, 7*

JANUARY 3
Pursuing a New Way

W E have come to know our Lord Jesus Christ, Who for our consolation was laid in a cramped and crowded lodging house and now, for our exaltation, is seated in heaven.

Let us proclaim Him in this land, in this region of our flesh, by not going back the way we came, nor seeking to follow in the footsteps of our former manner of life. That, after all, is the meaning of those Magi not going back the way they came. Change of way means change of life.
—*Sermon 202, 4*

PRAYER. *We acknowledge and praise You, Christ our Lord. You are king and priest and the One Who died for us.* —*Sermon 202, 4*

JANUARY 4
Let Us Celebrate the Birthday of the Form of a Slave

W E walk by faith and wander in exile from God, while we hunger and thirst for justice, and long with an ardor beyond words for the beauty of the form of God.

Let us express our allegiance by devoutly and loyally celebrating the birthday of the form of a slave.
—*Sermon 194,4*

PRAYER. *Lord, Your promise is that we should rejoice in Your countenance and gaze upon it.*
—*On Ps. 75, 1, 5*

JANUARY 5

We Have Christ as an Infant;
Let Us Grow Up with Him

HERE are You, O Lord Jesus, for my sake? In a cramped and crowded hostelry; in rags; in a manger.

He made Himself small, but didn't lose Himself; He took on what He was not, but remained what He was. There you are: we have Christ as an infant; let us grow up with Him.

—*Sermon 196, 3*

PRAYER. *O Food and Bread of angels! The angels take their fill of You; they derive their life from You; and where are You for my sake?*

—*Sermon 196, 3*

JANUARY 6

Cherish Eternal Life

HAT should be more dear to you than anything else is what you will reach after all your labors and never be in danger of losing.

If something is dear to you which you have reached after all your labors, and are certainly going to lose sooner or later, how much more should you desire what is everlasting?

—*Sermon 62, 16*

PRAYER. *Lord, grant me something eternal, something never dying. Give me wisdom, Your own Word, God with God.* —On Ps. 102, 1, 10

11

JANUARY 7
I Am with You through the Members

UR Head has now picked us up in His Body; where He is, the members of His Body will follow in due course because, where the Head has gone on ahead, the Body is bound to follow.

He is in heaven, we are on earth. If you question space, He is far away; if you question love, He is with us. —*Sermon 395, 2*

PRAYER. *How great is the consideration You show us, O good Lord. You Who made us came down to us.* — *Sermon 395, 2*

JANUARY 8
Christ Spoke from Heaven with a Star

HRIST couldn't yet speak with His tongue on earth, so He spoke from heaven with a star. Thus He demonstrated Who He was, and from where, and for whose sake He had come, not with the voice of flesh, but by the power of the Word which had become flesh. —*Sermon 202, 2*

PRAYER. *Say it, Lord, that I can hear it. My heart is listening; open the ears of my heart and say to my soul, "I am your salvation."*

—*Confessions I, 5, 5*

JANUARY 9
Catch Hold of God's Lowliness

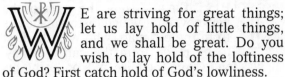E are striving for great things; let us lay hold of little things, and we shall be great. Do you wish to lay hold of the loftiness of God? First catch hold of God's lowliness.

Deign to be lowly and humble on the same account, yours, not His own. So catch hold of Christ's humility; learn to be humble; don't be proud. —*Sermon 117, 17*

PRAYER. *Let the haughty laugh at me, let them laugh who have never yet been flat on their faces, felled for their own good by You, my God.* — *Confessions IV, 1, 1*

JANUARY 10
Grasp Firmly What Will Give You a Firm Grasp of Things

ET it be charity that we gulp from the abundance of the spring, this that we take hold of, on this that we are nourished. Grasp firmly what will give you a firm grasp of things.

Let charity bring you to birth, charity rear you, charity perfect you, charity stiffen you, so that you may see the seeing of the Word, and that the Word is not one thing, and another His seeing; but that what the seeing of the Word is, that is what the Word is too. —*Sermon 126, 15*

PRAYER. *O my Lord, You will never cease to be the subject of my hymns and praises.*
—*Soliloquies of the Soul with God IV, 3*

JANUARY 11
Sing the New Song

THIS is the new song: the grace of the new covenant which distinguishes us from the old man, who was the first to be made from the earth, earthy. He was made from the mire and, on losing his happy state, was rightly cast forth into wretchedness because he had emerged as a transgressor of the commandment.

For none can praise God, that is utter a hymn, unless they tune their deeds to their words by loving God and neighbor.—*Sermon 33, 5*

PRAYER. *Let anyone who understands this praise You, O God, and anyone who does not understand it praise You no less.*

—*Confessions XI, 31, 41*

JANUARY 12
The Power of a Human Word

WHATEVER I speak, it's all there for all of you and all there for each of you. That's how it's impossible to explain satisfactorily the enormous power a human word has, and you ask me what the Word of God is?

Let Him tell us Himself, the only-begotten, the only Son. He put it very briefly but what He says is something tremendous: "I and the Father are one." —*Sermon 237, 4*

PRAYER. *I love only You, I follow only You, I seek for only You, and I am ready to serve only You.* —*Soliloquies I, 1, 5*

JANUARY 13
Do Not Be Ungrateful for Grace

E were all perfectly capable of wounding ourselves, but which of us is capable of curing what we've done. It's the same with misdeeds; any of you can wound yourselves, can't you, whenever you like? But you can't cure yourself whenever you like.

So have a God-fearing mind; be faithfully a Christian; do not be ungrateful for grace. Acknowledge the Doctor; the sick never cure themselves. —*Sermon 160, 7*

PRAYER. *Let me know You, O You Who know me; then shall I know even as I am known.*
—*Confessions X, 1, 1*

JANUARY 14
Beware of All Avarice

IVE me a person who has listened to Christ; give me a person who has listened in fear and trembling to the words, "Beware of all avarice."

Look at yourself inside, see what's inside you, examine what's inside you. Take your seat in judgment against yourself, set yourself before yourself and stretch yourself on the rack of God's commandment. Don't be soft on yourself; answer yourself. —*Sermon 107, 9*

PRAYER. *You wanted to show me first and foremost, O Lord, how You thwart the proud but give grace to the humble.*

—*Confessions VII, 9, 13*

JANUARY 15
Place Your Heart on High

LIFT up what you love on high, and love it there. And don't imagine you are only going to get back what you deposit.

You deposit perishable things; you will receive back imperishable. You deposit temporal things; you will get back eternal ones. You deposit earthly things; you will get back heavenly things. Finally, you hand out what your Lord has given you, and the reward you will receive from Him is your Lord Himself. —*Sermon 114A, 3*

PRAYER. *Give me what I love; for I love indeed, and this love You have given me, O God.*

—*Confessions XI, 22, 28*

JANUARY 16
We All Want Truth and Life

WHEN that rich man asked the Lord, "What good must I do to obtain eternal life?" the Lord told him to keep the commandments. He said, "I've done all that!"

But when He gave His answer about the commandments, what did the Lord say? "If you want to come to life. . . ." He didn't say "blessed life" because a wretched one isn't really to be called life. He didn't say "eternal life" because where there is fear of death it isn't really to be called life. —*Sermon 150, 10*

PRAYER. *Allow my soul to give You glory, Lord, that it may love You more.* —*Confessions V, 1, 1*

JANUARY 17

If You Walk along the Humble Christ, You Will Arrive at the Exalted Christ

 CHRIST "the way" is the humble Christ; Christ "the truth and life" is Christ the exalted and God. If you walk along the humble Christ, you will arrive at the exalted Christ; if, in your sickly health and debility, you do not spurn the humble One, you will abide in perfect health and strength with the exalted One.

What else, after all, was the reason for Christ's humility but your debility? Because you were not able to go to Him, He came to you. He came, teaching humility. —*Sermon 142, 2*

PRAYER. O Lord our God, grant us to trust in Your overshadowing wings; protect us beneath them and bear us up. —*Confessions IV, 16, 31*

JANUARY 18

The God I Worship

LOOK at Paul, not comprehending and yet seeking, following on behind, panting, sighing, longing; look at him, see what he's pointing at his God, what he's stretching out, whether it's a finger or his spirit.

I follow on, he says, I keep on walking, he says, I'm on the way. Follow on yourself, if you can. Let us come to our final home together where you won't seek answers from me, nor I from you. —*Sermon 261, 3*

PRAYER. Let us turn back to You at last, Lord, that we be not overturned. —*Confessions IV, 16, 31*

JANUARY 19
Filled with the Fullness of God

THINK of a tree; it fixes its roots in the lowly soil in order to stretch out its topmost branches to the sky.

You, though, wish to comprehend the heights without charity; you are challenging the winds without roots. That's the way to come crashing down, not to grow. With Christ dwelling in your hearts through faith, be rooted and grounded in love that you may be filled with all the fullness of God. —*Sermon 117, 17*

PRAYER. *Come, Lord, stir us and call us back, kindle us and seize us; let us love You and run to You.* —*Confessions VIII, 4, 9*

JANUARY 20
The Rich Man and the Poor Man

REMEMBER that rich man in the Gospel, and that poor man; that rich man clothed in purple and fine linen and stuffing himself with a feast every day; that poor man, on the other hand, lying before the rich man's gate, famished, begging for scraps from his table, covered with sores.

So you remember it; you can only remember it, can't you, because Christ is there in your hearts? —*Sermon 102, 3*

PRAYER. *O almighty and most loving Physician, wash my soul in the waters of tribulation; so that it might receive the imprint of Your image.* —*Soliloquies of the Soul with God II, 10*

JANUARY 21
In Praise of Charity

 HAT a great thing charity is! The soul of the Scriptures, the force of prophesy, the saving power of the Sacraments, the fruit of faith, the wealth of the poor, the life of the dying.

What could be more magnanimous than to die for the godless; what more kindly than to love one's enemies? —*Sermon 350, 3*

PRAYER. *Lord, give me more faith, more hope, more love.* —*Soliloquies I, 1, 5*

JANUARY 22
Pursue After Charity

 HARITY is the one thing that is not cast down by another's good fortune because it is not jealous. It is the one thing its own good fortune does not puff up because it is not conceited. It is the one thing that is not pricked by a bad conscience because it does not act boastfully.

It is steady and unshaken amid reproaches; it is well-disposed in the face of hatred, calm in the face of anger, innocent in the midst of intrigues, groaning in the midst of iniquity, breathing again in the presence of truth.

—*Sermon 350, 2*

PRAYER. *O Lord, I love You. I love, I burn, I pant for You; I trample under foot all that give here delight. I want to go to You.* —*Sermon 159, 8*

JANUARY 23

That We May Be the Justice of God in Him

CHRIST our Lord, Jesus our Savior, our Redeemer, was made into sin for us that we might be made the justice of God in Him. How? Listen to the law. In the law those sacrifices which were offered for sins were also called sins. And what else is Christ but the sacrifice for sin?

Paul says Christ loved you and gave Himself up for you as an offering and sacrifice to God for an odor of sweetness. So let one law show you what sin is and the other take it away. Let the law of the letter show you sin and the law of grace take it away. —*Sermon 152, 11*

PRAYER. *Let me know You, O You Who know me; then shall I know even as I am known.*

—*Confessions X, 1, 1*

JANUARY 24

The Lord Made Flesh Taught Those Who Believe in Him How To Live and How To Die

THIS Lord and Savior of ours, the Son of God, the Word of God Who became flesh, taught those who believe in Him how to live, taught them how to die: to live without greed, to die without fear.

He taught us how to live so that we might not die forever; He taught us how to die so that we might live forever. —*Sermon 313E, 1*

PRAYER. *Speak to me, O my God, within my heart in truth, for You alone speak so.*

—*Confessions XII, 16, 23*

JANUARY 25
You Are Persecuting Me

HEN Jesus cried out [to Paul] "You are persecuting Me," He was indicating that we are His members. And so may the love of Christ, Whom we love in you, the love of Christ, Whom you love in us, lead us all, among our trials, our temptations, our toils, our sweat, our anxieties, our misfortunes, to where there's no toil, no misfortune, no groans, no sighs, no vexations; where nobody's born, nobody dies, nobody has to fear the wrath of the mighty man, all being protected by the countenance of the Almighty God. —*Sermon 229N, 3*

PRAYER. *You pierced my heart, O God, with Your word, and I fell in love with You.*
—*Confessions X, 6, 8*

JANUARY 26
The Reason the World Hates Us Is That We, the Body of Christ, Preach Christ our Head

UR faith most truly holds that Jesus was sent to us as our Savior; since Christ is being preached by Christ Himself, that is, by the Body of Christ spread throughout the whole world.

So Christ is preaching Christ, the Body preaching its Head, and the Head looking after its Body. —*Sermon 354, 1*

PRAYER. *All those, O Lord, who rightly search for You, You have caused to search rightly for You.* —*Soliloquies I, 1, 6*

JANUARY 27
God Made Himself Our Debtor

GOD out of His goodness, not our rights, has become a debtor. What have we ever given Him, that we should be able to hold Him in our debt? Or perhaps because you heard in the psalm, "What shall I render to the Lord?"

They are the words of a debtor, not of someone demanding repayment of a debt. Something has been advanced to him. To begin with, I was nothing, and He made me.

—Sermon 254, 6

PRAYER. *O God, what shall I render to You for all the things You have rendered to me?*

—Sermon 254, 6

JANUARY 28
The Son of God Became the Way

THE Son of God, Who is always in the Father truth and life, became the way by taking to Himself a Man. Walk along the Man and you arrive at God.

You go by Him, you come to Him. Don't look for a way to come to Him apart from Him. After all, if He had refused to be the way, we would always be going astray. *—Sermon 141, 4*

PRAYER. *God, You lead us to the door; You cause it to be opened.* *—Soliloquies I, 1, 4*

JANUARY 29
Humble and Friendly in Giving

THE spirit of the person who actually hands something to the poor experiences a kind of sympathy with common humanity and infirmity when the hand of the one who has is actually placed in the hand of the one who is in need.

Although the one is giving, the other receiving, yet the one being attended to and the one attending are being joined in a real relationship. You see, it isn't calamity that really unites us, but humanity. —*Sermon 259, 5*

PRAYER. *O Lord my God, hear my prayer. May Your mercy hearken to my longing, a longing on fire not for myself alone but to serve the brethren I dearly love.* —*Confessions XI, 2, 3*

JANUARY 30
Son of God and Son of Man

THE Maker of man, He was made Man, so that the Director of the stars might be a Babe at the breast; that Bread might be hungry and the Fountain thirsty; that the Light might sleep and the Way be weary from a journey; that the Truth might be accused by false witnesses and the Judge of the living and the dead be judged by a mortal judge. —*Sermon 191, 1*

PRAYER. *O God, You made humanity in Your image and likeness; listen to me in that way of Yours known only to a few.* —*Soliloquies I, 1, 4*

JANUARY 31
Believe in the Divinity of Christ

HOLD on to the faith in all its strength and integrity and catholicity. Whenever you hear or read in the Scriptures a place where the Father is shown to be greater, remember "the form of a servant"; while when you read that Father and Son are one, believe the Divinity of Christ.

—*Sermon 229G*

PRAYER. *Remember, Lord, we are Your little flock: keep us as Your own. Spread Your wings and let us flee to shelter beneath them.*

—*Confessions X, 36, 59*

FEBRUARY 1
Conceive Christ in Faith, Give Birth to Him in Works

BECAUSE Christ is truth and peace and justice, conceive Him in faith, give birth to Him in works, so that what Mary's womb did for the flesh of Christ, your hearts may do for Christ's law.

How, I mean to say, can you have no part in Mary's childbearing when you are members of Christ? Mary gave birth to your Head, the Church to all of you.

—*Sermon 192, 2*

PRAYER. *I have never forgotten You because wherever I have found truth I have found You, my God.*

—*Confessions X, 24, 35*

FEBRUARY 2
Let Us Proclaim the Good News
of His Salvation

ET us proclaim the good news of "day from day, His salvation"; let us proclaim "among the nations His glory, among all the peoples His wonders."

He lies in the manger but holds the whole world in His hands; He sucks His Mother's breasts but feeds the angels; He is swaddled in rags but clothes us in immortality; He is suckled but also worshiped. —*Sermon 190, 4*

PRAYER. O Divine Word, we are filled with wonder at the virgin's bearing a child.

—*Sermon 192, 1*

FEBRUARY 3
Carried by Christ the Divine Being

ROCLAIM the good news of "day from day, his salvation." This, you see, is what Simeon was saying: "The One I was waiting for has come; what am I doing here any longer?"

He took Him, being on the point of being taken by Him. He was carrying Christ in human form; He was being carried by Christ the Divine Being. —*Sermon 217, 6*

PRAYER. What we marvel at in the flesh of Mary, help us, O God, to perform in the depths of our souls. —*Sermon 191, 4*

FEBRUARY 4
The Heavenly Bank

THE only, and the whole, profit to be made from riches, is treasure in the kingdom of heaven. That's why the Lord did not give the advice to throw your gold away but to transfer it to another bank.

He didn't tell you, did He: "When you give it away you lose it," but rather: "It's a bad investment for you on earth; I Myself will keep it safe for you in heaven." —*Sermon 15A, 5*

PRAYER. *O manifest infirmity and wondrous humility in which was thus concealed total Divinity!* —*Sermon 184, 3*

FEBRUARY 5
Difference between Eternity and Time

THERE is a considerable difference between eternity and time. Here devotion is required of you, there you take your rest. For this reason, like good traders, let us note every day how we have gotten on, what profit we have made.

We have not only to be attentive at listening but vigorously active as well. This is a school in which God is the only teacher, and it demands good students, those who are keen in attendance, not those who play truant. —*Sermon 16A, 1*

PRAYER. *My hope, Lord, is that You will bring Your merciful dealings in me to perfection.*

—*Confessions X, 30, 42*

FEBRUARY 6
True Piety

ET us show true piety in our lives. Let us love God freely and for nothing. He that has presented us on our journey with the form of a servant is reserving for our arrival at our final destination the form of God.

From the form of a servant He has constructed the roadway; from the form of God He has constituted His Father's kingdom.

—Sermon 91, 9

PRAYER. *Let us call upon God as God; love God as God. For You are full of mercy to those that call upon You.* *—On Ps. 85, 1*

FEBRUARY 7
Beholding God

HAT calls for all our efforts in this life is the healing of the eyes of our hearts, with which God is to be seen.

It is for this that the holy Mysteries are celebrated, for this that the word of God is preached, to this that the Church's moral exhortations are directed—those, that is, that are concerned with the correction of our carnal desires, the improvement of our habits, the renunciation of this world, not only in words but in a change of life. *—Sermon 88, 5*

PRAYER. *O God, You are truth and overflowing wealth of goodness that deceives not.*

—Confessions V, 12, 22

FEBRUARY 8
Let God Be Your Hope

VISIBLE things are delightful, they're beautiful, they're good; seek the One Who made them: He it is that is your hope. He it is that is now your hope, and He it is that will later on be the reality you will possess. Your hope while you believe, your possession when you see.

Let Him be your hope in the land of the dying, and He will be your portion in the land of the living. —*Sermon 313F, 3*

PRAYER. *Lord, my God, be my hope.*

—*On Ps. 39, 7*

FEBRUARY 9
Belief in Jesus Christ

THE medicine for all the wounds of the soul, and the one way of atoning for all human delinquency, is to believe in Christ. Nor is it in the least possible for any people to be cleansed . . . unless they are by faith joined and fitted to the Body of Him Who "committed no sin, neither was any trickery found in His mouth."

By believing in Him they become children of God, because they are born of God adoptively by the grace which consists of faith in Jesus Christ our Lord. —*Sermon 143, 1*

PRAYER. *Look upon my heart, O God, look upon this heart of mine, on which You took pity in its abysmal depths.* —*Confessions II, 4, 9*

FEBRUARY 10
Christ the Conqueror

AFTER the devil had completed every temptation, he departed from Him until the time. He departed from Him in the form, that is, of the "insidious serpent"; he is going to come in the form of the "roaring lion." But the One Who will trample on the lion and the dragon will conquer him. He will return; he will enter into Judas, will make him betray his Master; he will bring along the people, and he will cry out with the tongues of all of them, "Crucify Him, crucify Him!"

That Christ was the conqueror there, why should we be surprised? He was almighty God.

—*Sermon 284, 5*

PRAYER. *When I seek You, my God, what I am seeking is a life of happiness.*

—*Confessions X, 20, 29*

FEBRUARY 11
Friends Should Be Freely Loved

FRIENDS are to be loved freely, for their own sake, not for the sake of something else. If the rule of friendship urges you to love others freely, for their own sakes, how much more freely is God to be loved Who bids you love them! There can be nothing more delightful than God. —*Sermon 385, 4*

PRAYER. *Blessed is the one who loves You, Lord, and loves his friend in You.*

—*Confessions IV, 9, 14*

FEBRUARY 12
Make Your Choice Now

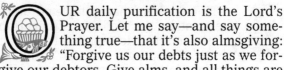

UR daily purification is the Lord's Prayer. Let me say—and say something true—that it's also almsgiving: "Forgive us our debts just as we forgive our debtors. Give alms, and all things are pure for you."

Remember what He is going to say to those who will be standing on the right. He won't say: "You've done this and that great deed" but: "I was hungry and you gave Me to eat."

—*Sermon 261, 9*

PRAYER. *Help us, Lord, to abound in good works, in kindness, in goodness, in generosity.*
—*Sermon 261, 9*

FEBRUARY 13
I Can't Show You My God;
I Can Show You What He Made

OVE God; whatever you love it comes from Him. Don't let us love the creature to the neglect of the Creator, but let us pay attention to the creature and praise the Creator.

I can't show you my God; I can show you what He made. I can remind you of what He made. All things were made through Him.

—*Sermon 261, 4*

PRAYER. *The mercy, O God, You lavish on Your holy ones is a heavenly, not an earthly, mercy.* —*On Ps. 35, 8*

FEBRUARY 14

Not All Will Have a Place in Christ's Kingdom

MANY people receive the Sacrament of Christ's Body, but not all who receive the Sacrament are also going to have the place in His company promised to His members. Nearly all people, indeed, say the Sacrament is His Body because all are feeding together in His pastures.

But He is going to come and separate them and place some on the right, some on the left. And each section is going to say: "Lord, Lord, when did we see You and minister to You?" or else: "Lord, when did we see You and not minister to You?"
—Sermon 354, 2

PRAYER. *Command me, I beg You, and make any decree You wish, but heal and open my ears, so that I may hear Your voice.*
—Soliloquies I, 1, 5

FEBRUARY 15

What Is Repentance?

WHAT is repentance but being angry with oneself? What is the idea of beating your breast if you are not just pretending? Why beat it if you are not angry with it?

So when you beat your breast you are being angry with your heart in order to make amends to your Lord.
—Sermon 19, 2

PRAYER. *O God, let us give our heart a shaking by repentance, and this will be our sacrifice to You.*
—Sermon 19, 2

FEBRUARY 16
Let Us Give in Order To Receive

IF IT'S shameless of a farmer to look for a crop where he knows he hasn't sown any seed, how much more shameless must it be to look to God to be rich in giving when you have declined to listen to a poor man asking? It's in the poor man, after all, that the One Who is never hungry has wished to be fed.

Let us not, then, spurn our God when He is needy in the poor so that we, in our need, may be satisfied by Him in His riches. We have needy people, and we are needy ourselves; so let us give in order to receive. —*Sermon 206, 2*

PRAYER. *O God, we have found You trustworthy; You will care for us.* —*On Ps. 39, 8*

FEBRUARY 17
Fasting and Feasting

FASTING represents the pains of the contest, since "anyone who enters the contest is abstemious in all things." Food, on the other hand, represents the hope of peace—which will not be perfect until our bodies, whose redemption we are awaiting, "have put on immortality."

We don't yet glory in the acquisition of this but are already being fed on the hope of it.

—*Sermon 263A, 4*

PRAYER. *Without You, O God, all to me is misery, woe outside myself and woe within, and all wealth but penury, if it is not You, my God.* —*Confessions XIII, 8, 9*

FEBRUARY 18
Recollect Who You Are

ECOLLECT how, and as to what sort of creature, you came. It was here that you came into everything. And if you misuse the fortune you have come into, it only means you have swollen up with pride. Didn't you come naked out of your mother's womb?

Give, therefore, give, in order not to lose what you have. If you give you are going to find it waiting for you there; if you don't give you are going to leave it behind here. —*Sermon 114A, 4*

PRAYER. *I love You, O God, but if my love is too mean, let me love more passionately.*

—*Confessions XIII, 8, 9*

FEBRUARY 19
Let Us Be on the Watch

E should fight to the death for truth and never give false evidence, never perjure ourselves, but stick to the path of justice even when it is dangerous. There is nothing very remarkable, after all, in sticking to the path of justice when it's perfectly safe to do so.

Let us always bear in mind that the devil is on the watch against us, our tempter and our persecutor; and, in the name and with the help of the Lord our God, let us be the more ardently on the watch. —*Sermon 94A, 5*

PRAYER. *It is You, Lord, Who will light up our darkness.* —*Confessions XIII, 8, 9*

FEBRUARY 20

You Will Be Full of God

RECOGNIZE and love the One Who made you, and He will fill you with Himself. You will possess God; you will be full of God. This is the great wealth of the soul. The wealth of the body is superfluous because our bodies require little enough to manage. The wealth of the soul is not superfluous.

Your inner riches are enormous. O poor one, do you think you have nothing if you have God? O rich one, do you think you have anything if you don't have God? —*Sermon 107A, 3*

PRAYER. *Lord, open the ears of my heart and say to my soul, "I am your salvation." Let me run toward this voice and seize hold of You.*

—*Confessions I, 5, 5*

FEBRUARY 21

The Creator from Heaven!

WHAT greater mercy could there be toward the miserable than that which pulled the Creator down from heaven and clothed the Founder of the earth in an earthly body!

This made the One Who abides equal in eternity to the Father, equal to us in mortality, imposing the form of a servant on the Lord of the world; so that Bread itself would be hungry, Fullness would be thirsty, Strength would become weak, Health would be wounded, and Life would die! —*Sermon 207, 1*

PRAYER. *You, Lord, have blotted out all the evils in me.* —*Confessions XIII, 1, 1*

FEBRUARY 22

The Keys of the Church Are More Dependable than the Hearts of Kings

HAT do you lose when you beseech God for pardon, seeing that you didn't hesitate to lose your spiritual health when you offended God? Who can be certain, after all, that the emperor will grant a pardon either?

Still, money is poured out, seas are crossed, the uncertainty of storms are braved, and, to avoid death, death itself is practically experienced! Yet the keys of the Church are more dependable than *the hearts of kings.*—Sermon 351, 12

PRAYER. *Over all that I am, Your goodness, O God, has absolute precedence.*

—Confessions XIII, 1, 1

FEBRUARY 23

Fasting and Feasting

ASTING represents the pains of the contest. Food represents the hope of peace—which will not be perfect until our bodies, whose redemption we are awaiting, have "put on immortality."

We don't yet glory in its acquisition but are already being fed on the hope of it. While traveling the way of the Lord, we should be fasting from the vanity of the present age, and feasting on the promise of the age to come.   —Sermon 263A, 4

PRAYER. *You, Lord, have told us that You are with us until the consummation of the world.*

—Sermon 263A, 4

FEBRUARY 24

The Time of Faith Is Toilsome

THE time of faith is toilsome, but this is the work for which there is payment. Don't be lazy at the work for which you desire payment.

If you yourself had hired a workman, you wouldn't count out his pay before you had put him to work. You would say to him: "Do it, then you'll get it." So it's the same with God. You, being a God-fearing person, do not cheat your worker. —*Sermon 38, 4*

PRAYER. *Speak to me Yourself, Lord, within my heart in truth, for You alone speak so.*

—*Confessions XII, 16, 23*

FEBRUARY 25

Avarice and Extravagance

SOMETIMES two opposing mistresses take possession of a person: Avarice says: "Save"; Extravagance says: "Spend." Under two such mistresses, giving contradictory orders, making contradictory demands, what are you going to do?

Grow weary, O free people called to freedom, of enslavement to such mistresses. Recognize and acknowledge your Redeemer, your Liberator. Be His slaves; He gives you easier commands, not contradictory commands.

—*Sermon 86, 7*

PRAYER. *Lord, help us to be on our guard against the coaxing avarice and extravagance.*

—*Sermon 86, 6*

FEBRUARY 26
Peace

THE time when our external enemy, the devil, will be under our feet is when the internal enemy, covetousness, has been healed and we shall be living in peace.

What sort of peace? The sort about which the Apostle said, "The peace of God which passes all understanding keep your hearts."

—*Sermon 77A, 2*

PRAYER. *O Lord our God, give us peace; for You have given us everything You promised.*

—*Sermon 77A, 2*

FEBRUARY 27
Our Prayer Seeks Peace and Obtains It

IN humility and charity, by fasting and giving, by restraining ourselves and pardoning, by paying out good deeds and not paying back bad ones, by turning away from evil and doing good, our prayer seeks peace and obtains it.

Prayer, you see, flies beautifully when it's supported on wings of such virtues and is in this way more readily wafted through to heaven, where Christ our peace has preceded us.

—*Sermon 206, 3*

PRAYER. *I come back to You, O God, fevered and panting for Your fountain. Let no one bar my way; let me drink it and draw life from it.*

—*Confessions XII, 10, 10*

FEBRUARY 28
The Lord of the Press Knows His Oil

 OMETHING is always going on in this olive press. The world is the press—there is no end to its pressures. Be oil, not dregs. Let each of you be converted to God and change your manner of life.

The Lord of the press does not cease from operating it through His workers, the holy angels. He knows His oil, He knows how much it can take, the exact pressure needed to squeeze it out. The Lord, you see, knows His own.

—Sermon 19, 6

PRAYER. *You enable me, Lord, and urge me to knock, and open to my knocking.*

—Confessions XII, 12, 15

FEBRUARY 29
What God Made in Us Is Good

 OD sent His Son to redeem us. We have received this grace. Let us live worthily of what we have received. Let us do no wrong to so great a grace.

Such a splendid Doctor has come to us! He has forgiven all our sins. If we are determined to get sick again, we shall not only be very damaging to ourselves but also ungrateful to the Doctor.

—Sermon 23A, 2

PRAYER. *Make me, Father, search for You and protect me from evil; and as I search, let there be nothing else for me other than You.*

—Soliloquies I, 1, 6

MARCH 1

Even Sinners Are To Be Treated
with Human Consideration

 LMSGIVING, which is not to be made light of, is bestowed on any poor person by right of humanity, seeing that the Lord Himself relieved the wants of the poor even from those funds which were supplied from other people's contributions.

The most dastardly of sinners are, of course, those who hate and persecute the Church, and yet about them we are told: "Do good to those who hate you." And this is supported by the example of God the Father "Who makes His sun rise on the good and the bad, and sends His rain on the just and the unjust."   —*Sermon 164A, 4*

PRAYER. *Help us, Lord, to be tireless in doing good.*   —*Sermon 164A, 4*

MARCH 2

Taking Inventory of Charity

 UBMIT yourselves, my dear brothers and sisters, to a thorough investigation, turn out your innermost closets and cupboards.

Take careful stock of how much you have of charity—and increase the stock you find. Pay attention to that sort of treasure so that you may be rich within.   —*Sermon 34, 7*

PRAYER. *May we find charity in ourselves, Lord.*   —*Sermon 34, 7*

MARCH 3
Fighting Temptation

UNTIL we come to that peace where we shall have no enemies, we must go on fighting long and faithfully and strenuously in order to earn the victor's crown from the Lord God.

The Apostle James says: "Let no one say when they are tempted that they are being tempted by God." —*Sermon 77A, 3*

PRAYER. *From out of eternity on high You are waiting for the sinner's day to pass so that the time of the just may come. For Your enemies will perish, O Lord, Your enemies will perish.* —*On Ps. 91, 7*

MARCH 4
Desiring Inward Healing

WE need to get hold of the Doctor Who came for the diseases of the soul. But He was also willing to heal the diseases of the body precisely to show that He was the Savior and Healer of the spirit, because He is the Creator of each.

It's not the case, you see, that He is the Creator of the spirit and not of the body, and that's why He wanted to encourage the soul to get itself healed inwardly. —*Sermon 63A, 2*

PRAYER. *O almighty and most loving Physician, use all my miseries for the salvation of my soul.* —*Soliloquies II, 10*

MARCH 5

Denying Oneself in Love for Christ

SINCE most people are like the loves that drive them, and since their own concern in determining how they ought to live should only be to choose what they should love: why be surprised if those who love Christ and want to follow Christ should deny themselves in loving Him?

If you get lost through loving yourself, you get found in denying yourself. —*Sermon 96, 1*

PRAYER. *You, O God, show Yourself to anyone who loves You according to Your bidding.*
—*Confessions XII, 15, 19*

MARCH 6

My Word and the Word of God

JUST as my word was presented to your perception and didn't depart from my mind, so that Word was presented to our perception and didn't depart from His Father. My word was with me and went out in the sound of my voice; the Word of God was with the Father and went out in the flesh.

But I can hardly do with my voice what He did with His flesh, can I? I cannot hold onto my voice, I mean, as it flies away from me. He not only held on to His flesh, to be born, to live, to act in it, but also raised it up when it was dead. —*Sermon 119, 7*

PRAYER. *Your word, O God, is a fountain of eternal life which never passes away.*
—*Confessions XIII, 21, 31*

MARCH 7
Christ's Load Is a Relief To Carry

THE one who carries a heavy load appears to be weighed down, but still feels some weight; but the one who carries no load at all is evidently walking along with shoulders completely free.

Well, Christ's load is not like that at all. It's a relief, you see, to carry so that you can be lifted up and lightened. If you put it down, you find yourself more weighed down than ever. —*Sermon 112A, 6*

PRAYER. *How can we be capable of carrying You, O God, unless You, being carried, carry us?* —*Sermon 112A, 6*

MARCH 8
Attend to the Hungry Christ

YOU are all looking forward to greeting Christ, seated in heaven. Attend to Him lying under the arches, attend to Him hungry, attend to Him shivering with cold, attend to Him needy, attend to Him a foreigner. Do it if it's already your practice; do it if it isn't your practice.

Knowledge of Christian doctrine is growing; let good works grow too. You praise the Sower: present Him with a harvest. —*Sermon 25, 8*

PRAYER. *Christ, read me out the New Testament. Make us happy from Your law.*

—*Sermon 25, 8*

MARCH 9
The Tongue

WE have a great need of the tongue. What do we do with such a useful member? With it we pray to God, with it we make amends, with it we utter praises, with it we sing with one voice in harmony to God, with it every day we show ourselves kind and considerate when we talk to others or give them advice.

At this very moment, this very tongue of mine is performing you a service. —*Sermon 16A, 2*

PRAYER. *Open the lips of my heart so that its voice may exalt to the skies Your loving-kindness and infinite mercy.*

—*Book of Soliloquies of God VII, 2*

MARCH 10
The Way of Humility

HOW did Christ humble Himself? John himself tells us: The Word became flesh and dwelt among us. Being immortal He took on mortality in order to die for us and by His death kill our death.

This is what the Lord did; this is what He offered us. Being great He humbled Himself, being humbled He was killed, killed and risen and lifted up on high in Himself in the resurrection of the dead, having lifted us up now in faith and in the confession of the just. —*Sermon 23A, 4*

PRAYER. *Let Your merciful dealings themselves sing praise to You from the innermost depths of my soul, O my God.* —*Confessions VII, 6, 8*

MARCH 11

Forgive, and You Will Be Forgiven

LET there be in mild-mannered and humble spirits a compassionate ease in forgiving. Let the one who has done an injury ask pardon; let the one who has suffered an injury grant pardon; so that we may not be possessed by Satan, whose triumph is the discord of Christians.

And this, you see, is an alms deed of great value and profit: to forgive your fellow servant a debt so that you may be released from your debts by the Lord. —*Sermon 210, 12*

PRAYER. *Merciful Father, You are more joyful over one repentant sinner than over ninety-nine righteous people who need no repentance.*

—*Confessions VIII, 3, 6*

MARCH 12

Temptation

IN both the good things and the bad things of this world, in all of them temptation is to be met. The good things are liable to deceive us with their blandishments, the bad things to break us with their menace.

So because temptation is to be met in both sorts, the Christian is never wholly safe but must say and do with a whole heart what we have just been singing to God: "Have mercy on me, Lord, have mercy on me, for in You has my soul put its trust." —*Sermon 20A, 1*

PRAYER. *Have mercy on me, O God, for in You my soul has put its trust.* —*Sermon 20A, 1*

MARCH 13
Forgiveness Will Help Us To Live

I F you recall that you have neglected to make up with someone, then wake up and shake off your torpor. If you are so keen to exact payment from your debtor, just think for a moment that you are God's debtor.

If you are ashamed to ask someone to forgive you, overcome this bad sort of shame with a good sort of fear so that, with destructive animosities terminated, with them finally dead, you yourselves may live. —*Sermon 209, 1*

PRAYER. *From no place are You absent, Lord, yet how tardily do we return to You!*
—*Confessions VII, 3, 8*

MARCH 14
Recall Your Faith

C HRISTIAN, Christ is asleep in your boat. Wake Him up; He will command the storm, and everything will be calm.

What does it mean to wake up Christ? Waking up your faith, remembering what you have believed. So then, recall your faith, and wake up Christ. Your very faith will command the waves you are being troubled by and the winds of persuasive perversity. —*Sermon 361, 7*

PRAYER. *My faith calls upon You, Lord, this faith which is Your gift to me.* —*Confessions I, 1, 1*

MARCH 15
Let God Be Enough for You

LET God be enough for you for He does not desert you. He thought about you before you existed, and will He not think about you so that you can stay alive?

You have already come to believe in Him, you have praised Him, you have placed your hope in Him, and will you lack what He knows we all need? —*Sermon 107A, 5*

PRAYER. *O Lord our God, grant us to trust in Your overshadowing wings: protect us beneath them and bear us up. When You are our strong security, that is strength indeed.*

—*Confessions IV, 16, 31*

MARCH 16
Hold On to the Deformed Christ

IN this life let us hold on to the deformed Christ. What do I mean, the "deformed Christ"? "Far be it from me to boast except in the Cross of our Lord Jesus Christ, through Whom the world has been crucified to me, and I to the world." That's the deformed Christ.

Did I ever say I knew anything among you except the road? This is the road: to believe in the Crucified. We carry the sign of this deformity on our foreheads. —*Sermon 27, 6*

PRAYER. *Lord, Your deformity was our beauty.*

—*Sermon 27, 6*

MARCH 17
Forge Ahead

FORGE ahead, my brothers and sisters; always examine yourselves without self-deception, without flattery, without buttering yourselves up. After all, there's nobody inside you before whom you need feel ashamed or whom you need to impress.

There is Someone there, but He is One Who is pleased with humility. Let Him test you. And you, too, test yourselves. Always be dissatisfied with what you are if you want to arrive at what you are not yet. —*Sermon 169, 18*

PRAYER. *Help us, Lord, to keep on walking to forge ahead.* —*Sermon 169, 18*

MARCH 18
Even Now the Fire Is Burning

GOD made man, and man made sin. So why start trembling when God says to you: "Let sinners perish from before My face"? What God is saying to you is: "Let that perish in you which you made, and I will preserve what I made."

Even now the fire is burning, the heat of the word is on, the fierce glow of the Holy Spirit.
—*Sermon 22, 7*

PRAYER. *Lord, may I treat Your Scripture as Your face. May I melt in front of it.*

—*Sermon 22, 7*

MARCH 19
Joseph's Justice

HAT a just man indeed Joseph is! He doesn't keep an adulterous wife in case he should seem to spare her because he loves her in a lustful manner. And yet he neither punishes her nor exposes her to shame.

Rightly indeed was he chosen to bear witness to his wife's virginity. So while he was made uneasy by human weakness, he was reassured by Divine authority. —*Sermon 51, 9*

PRAYER. *Lord, give me the insight to understand that justice of which good and holy people are the servants.* —*Confessions III, 7, 14*

MARCH 20
Glory and Humility

UR Creator was subjected to us because He showed Himself as we are, our Liberator. He was subjected to us but in our form; hidden as God, showing Himself as human; despised as human, discovered as God; only discovered, however, because previously despised.

For, you see, He wasn't prepared to give you glory until He had first taught you humility.

—*Sermon 20A, 4*

PRAYER. *O God, You sent Your Son that by His example we might learn even a humility like His.* —*Confessions X, 43, 68*

MARCH 21
Go Along with a Humble God

I F we were to attempt to explain what lesson in patience is to be found in the Cross, or how salutary it is, what words could do justice to the subject, what time suffice for the words? Could anyone, I mean, who genuinely and seriously believes in Christ, have the audacity to be proud, when God teaches humility not only by word but by example?

How useful this lesson is, though, the following sentence from Holy Scripture briefly assures us: "Before ruin the heart is lifted up, and before glory it is humbled." —*Sermon 218C, 4*

PRAYER. *O God, Your only Son, in Whom are hidden all treasures of wisdom and knowledge, has redeemed me with His Blood.*

—*Confessions X, 43, 70*

MARCH 22
Repentance Is a Gift from God

T O wash away the sin of denial Peter needed the baptism of tears from the Lord. Paul gave this advice to his people about those with deviant opinions and about how they should deal with them:

"With gentleness correct those who have deviant opinions in case, perhaps, the Lord may give them repentance." So even repentance is a gift from God. —*Sermon 229O, 1*

PRAYER. *O God, the heart of the proud is softened for repentance if it is rained on by Your grace.* —*Sermon 229O, 1*

49

MARCH 23
In Exile Away from Christ

BLESSED were those who were privileged to have Jesus present among them before His Passion, to ask Him whatever they liked, and to listen to Him as they ought to listen.

Indeed we believe in Him as He is now seated at the right hand of the Father; and yet as long as we are in the body we are wandering in exile away from Him. *—Sermon 210, 4-5*

PRAYER. *Come, Lord, let us love You and run to You.* *—Confessions VIII, 4, 9*

MARCH 24
Grant Pardon to Your Fellow Human Beings

WHOEVER you are who give a thought to Christ and long to receive what He promised, do not be slow to do what He told you.

After all, what did He promise? Eternal life. And what did He tell you to do? Grant to your fellow human beings pardon. As though He were saying to you, "You, a human being, see that you grant pardon to your fellow human beings, so that I, God, may come to you."

—Sermon 114, 2

PRAYER. *Let it be out of love for loving You that I do this.* *—Confessions XI, 1, 1*

MARCH 25
The Word Is Made in the Womb of Mary

THE One Who made you is made in you, O Mary, the One through Whom you were made is made in you. Or rather, the One through Whom heaven and earth were made, through Whom all things were made, the Word of God, is made flesh in you, by receiving flesh, not by losing Divinity.

And the Word is united to flesh; the Word is coupled with flesh; and the bridal chamber of this astonishing marriage is your womb.

—Sermon 291, 6

PRAYER. *May Christ, the Virgin's Son, O God, born in the flesh of a virginal womb, come to my assistance.* *—Holy Virginity 100, 2*

MARCH 26
Both Had Riches: Humility

BECAUSE the same thing was found in the poor man Lazarus as in the rich man Abraham, namely humility, neither riches were a hindrance to the one nor poverty to the other, but the merit of both was their piety.

That's why with the rich man whose affairs took such a change for the worse, it wasn't his riches that were blamed but his attitude.

—Sermon 15A, 5

PRAYER. *O God, how high and glorious You are, yet You make the humble-hearted Your home!* *—Confessions XI, 31, 41*

MARCH 27
Heed the Warnings of Our Instructor

LET us all have the good sense to heed the warnings of our instructor and so not waste the time of the mercy of our Savior which is being spread out for us now, as long as the human race is being spared.

The reason, you see, we are being spared is so that we may be converted and there may be no one to be condemned.

—Sermon 109, 1

PRAYER. *My eyes are fixed on Your mercy, Lord.* *—Confessions X, 34, 53*

MARCH 28
Walk Securely in Christ

CHRIST became the way for us, and do we despair of arriving? This way cannot be closed, cannot be cut, cannot be broken up by rain or floods, nor blocked by bandits.

Walk securely in Christ, without anxiety. Walk! Don't stumble, don't fall, don't look back, don't wander away from the road. Only beware of all these things, and you have arrived. *—Sermon 170, 11*

PRAYER. *Lord, let us not move away from the warmth of the Spirit, from the light of the Truth.* *—Sermon 170, 11*

MARCH 29

Let Us Sow Our Souls in This Time

L ET us do what we were just singing about. Let us sow our souls in this time, like corn in winter, so that we may reap them in eternal time, like corn in summer.

That was the way the holy martyrs, the way all the just, toiling away on earth, weeping, cast their seed. This life, after all, is full of tears. But what follows? "But coming, they will come with exaltation, carrying their lapfuls." —*Sermon 313D, 3*

PRAYER. *Lord, our seed is the shedding of Your Blood, our lapful the reception of Your crown.* —*Sermon 313D, 3*

MARCH 30

Forgive as I Forgive

T HE terms have been stated, the rule fixed: "Forgive as I forgive." So He won't forgive unless you forgive. "Forgive as I forgive." You want forgiveness when you seek it; forgive anyone who seeks it from you.

These prayers were dictated by the heavenly law: say "Forgive, as we also forgive." And do what you say. If you lie in your prayers, you derive no benefit. —*Sermon 114, 5*

PRAYER. *Hear me, O God, through that healing Remedy Who hung upon the tree, the Medicine for our wounds Who sits at Your right hand and intercedes for us.*

—*Confessions IX, 13, 35*

MARCH 31
Ask, Seek, and Knock with Your Morals

ASK, seek, knock; you will receive; you will find; the door will be opened to you. Only don't just ask, seek, and knock with your voices but also with your morals. Do good works, without which you certainly have no business to lead this life.

Wipe out your sins by daily good works. Not even slight sins are to be treated lightly. They are nothing very big, of course, but they do pile up, they make a heap. Don't shrug them aside.

—*Sermon 77B, 7*

PRAYER. *Let us, Lord, ask of You, seek in You, knock at Your door.* —*Confessions XIII, 38, 53*

APRIL 1
We Should Take No Pride in Anything but the Cross

THIS is Christian teaching, the rule of humility, the recommendation of humility, that we should not take pride in anything except the Cross of our Lord Jesus Christ. After all, there's nothing special about taking pride in Christ's wisdom; there is something very special about taking pride in Christ's Cross.

Don't be ashamed or embarrassed about the Cross of Christ; that's why you received the sign on your forehead, as on a seat of shame.

—*Sermon 160, 5*

PRAYER. *Help us, O God, to remember what we have on our forehead.* —*Sermon 160, 5*

APRIL 2
The Lord Looked Round

READ the Gospel. The Lord was being tried in the interior of the house; Peter was being tested in the courtyard. So "the Lord looked round at him," not in the body but in Divine Majesty, not with a glance of His bodily eyes but with His sovereign mercy.

Having turned away His face, He looked round at Peter and he became liberated. So the one who was self-assured would have perished if the Redeemer had not looked round.

—Sermon 284, 6

PRAYER. *O God, You shed the light of salvation on my face.* *—Confessions X, 23, 33*

APRIL 3
Jesus Came To Die

THE One Whom the virgin conceived without lust, Whom she bore as a virgin and remained a virgin, the One Who lived without fault, Who did not die for any fault, Who shared the punishment with us and did not share the fault: the Lord Jesus Christ came to die; He did not come to sin.

By sharing with us the punishment without any fault, He released us from both fault and punishment. *—Sermon 231, 2*

PRAYER. *On the Cross, Lord, You demonstrate the downfall of our old self.* *—Sermon 231, 2*

APRIL 4
Jesus Came Down to Us; He Did Not Fall

DEATH in our Lord was a sign of alien sins, not a penalty for His own. In all other human beings, though, mortality is a penalty for sin; it is derived from the very origin of sin from which we all come: from the fall of that man, not from the coming down of this One.

It's one thing, I mean, to fall, another to come down. The one fell out of wickedness, the Other came down out of kindness.

—Sermon 361, 16

PRAYER. *You, Lord Jesus Christ, brought Divinity with You, but took on mortality for us.*

—Sermon 361, 16

APRIL 5
Christ Rose Again in What He Took from Us

WHY, by praising my Lord, do you wish to pull down the faith which my Lord built up in me? It's as a result of His taking the form of a servant that He died. But He rose again in the same respect as He died.

So I certainly need not despair in the least about the resurrection of a servant, since it was in the form of a servant that the Lord rose again. *—Sermon 361, 17*

PRAYER. *You rose, Lord, in order to demonstrate in Your life the newness of our own.*

—Sermon 231, 2

APRIL 6
Die, in Order Not To Die

F we live good lives, we have died and risen again. But any who have not died and risen again are still living bad lives. If they are living bad lives, then they are not, in fact, alive.

Let them die in order not to die. What's that? Let them die in order not to die? Let them change their ways in order not to be damned. —*Sermon 231, 3*

PRAYER. *May we live good lives, Lord, so that we may live again.* —*Sermon 231, 3*

APRIL 7
ted Us though Rejected Himself

HE only Son of God made many sons and daughters of God. He bought Himself brothers and sisters with His Blood; He accepted us though rejected Himself; He redeemed us though sold Himself; He did us honor though dishonored Himself; He gave us life though slain Himself.

Can you doubt that He will give you good things, seeing that He did not decline to take ad things? —*Sermon 171, 5*

PRAYER. *May we rejoice in truth, O God, not in iniquity.* —*Sermon 171, 5*

57

APRIL 8
Let Us Not Look Back

LET us not look back at what we were before Christ bought us in case we should remain stuck on the road. Let us not look back and, at the same time, though, let us keep it in remembrance.

If we look back, we return to it; if we forget it, we will be ungrateful. So it's good both to remember what we were and to hate it; to remember it in order to give thanks, to hate it in order not to return to old ways. —*Sermon 335I, 2*

PRAYER. *Strengthen me, Lord, and my heart will remain fixed on You.* —*On Ps. 85*

APRIL 9
Don't Collapse under Your Cross

WHAT does "take up their cross" mean? Let them bear with whatever is troublesome. You see, when they begin to follow Me in their manner of life and by keeping My commandments, they will find many speaking against them, many telling them to stop, many trying to dissuade them—and among them apparent companions of Christ.

If you want to follow Him, turn them into your Cross; endure it, carry it, don't collapse under it. —*Sermon 96, 4*

PRAYER. *Consider these loving and glorious tokens of Your promises, Lord, and create me anew in Your image and likeness.*—*Soliloquies II, 3*

APRIL 10

Hold On to the Death of Christ as Your Guarantee

ESIRE and long for the life of Christ that has been granted you and, until you get there, hold on to the death of Christ as your guarantee.

He couldn't, after all, have given us a greater guarantee when He promised He was going to live with us than to die for us. "I have borne," He says, "your evils. Will I not pay you back My good things?" —*Sermon 334, 2*

PRAYER. *I ask for eternal life. O hear me since it is Your own right hand I am asking for.*

—*On Ps. 59*

APRIL 11

Joy in the World

HAT is joy in the world? Rejoicing in iniquity, rejoicing in infamy, rejoicing in what is dishonorable, rejoicing in what is vile. These are all things that the world rejoices in. And none of them would exist if people didn't want them to. There are some things that people do, others that are done to them. They endure even if they don't like it.

So what is this world, and what is the joy of this world? What the world relishes is villainy that no one punishes. —*Sermon 171, 4*

PRAYER. *O Lord my God, You are Yourself Your own eternal joy, and all around You heaven rejoices in You eternally.* —*Confessions VIII, 3, 8*

APRIL 12
Risen from the Dead

ET us believe in Christ crucified, but in Him as the One Who rose again on the third day. That's the faith that distinguishes us. That is the salvation, the well-being, the safety and the soundness. Whoever believes and is baptized shall be saved.

I know you believe; you will be saved. Hold firmly in your hearts, profess it with your lips, that Christ has risen from the dead.

—Sermon 234, 3

PRAYER. *Lord, I believe in Christ risen from the dead.* *—Sermon 234, 2*

APRIL 13
The Ardor of Love Seeks the Heights

HATEVER vexations you suffer on earth, however much the enemy may humiliate Christian hearts and press them downward, the ardor of love seeks the heights.

Here's a comparison for you. If you're holding a burning torch, holding it upright with its head on top, the flame, like hair, surges up toward the sky; lower the torch, and the flame goes up to the sky; turn the torch upside down, and do you also push the flame down to the earth? Wherever the burning brand is turned, the flame knows no other road but to seek the sky. *—Sermon 234, 3*

PRAYER. *Lord, may we set ourselves alight with the fire of charity.* *—Sermon 234, 2*

APRIL 14
Be Filled with the Holy Spirit

THE Holy Spirit has just begun to live in you; don't let Him quit, don't shut Him out of your hearts. He's a good guest: He found you empty, and He fills you; He found you hungry, and He feeds you; and He found you thirsty, and He makes you drunk.

Let Him make you drunk because the Apostle says: "Do not get drunk on wine, which leads to all kind of debauchery"—and to teach us what we should get drunk on, he says—"but be filled with the Holy Spirit." —*Sermon 225, 4*

PRAYER. *Fill us, Lord, with Your Holy Spirit.*

—*Sermon 225, 4*

APRIL 15
The Exodus and the Desert Journey

YOU must think of yourselves as brought out of Egypt, freed from harsh slavery, in which iniquity was your master; as having also passed through the Red Sea through baptism, which was marked by the bloodstained Cross of Christ.

As for the enemies pursuing you from behind: consider them to be your past sins because, just as the Egyptians perished when the people of God passed through, so were your sins obliterated when you were baptized. —*Sermon 260B, 1*

PRAYER. *Help us, Lord, to cling with steadfast obedience to You Who redeemed us.*

—*Sermon 260B, 3*

APRIL 16
Touch and Believe

OUR Lord says, "Come, touch, and believe. You said: 'Unless I touch, unless I put my finger in, I will not believe.' Come, touch, 'put in your fingers and do not be unbelieving but trusting.' Come, put in your finger. I was aware of your wounds, I preserved My scars especially for you."

—Sermon 258, 3

PRAYER. *Lord, we believe that Christ is both Man and God.*

—Sermon 258, 3

APRIL 17
Let Us All Run in the Tracks of the Lord

WE instruct you with sermons; it is up to you to make progress in your conduct. We scatter the seed of the word; it is up to you to produce the crop of faith.

Let us all run the course in the tracks of the Lord according to the vocation with which we have been called by Him; none of us must look back. Truth, you see, Who can neither be misled nor mislead, openly warns us: "Nobody putting hand to plow and looking back is fit for the kingdom of heaven." *—Sermon 216, 1*

PRAYER. *Why do you put off listening to Him Who is calling you? See that by your delay you do not deprive yourself of His promises!*

—Sermon 87, 7

APRIL 18
Choose for Yourselves the Ones To Imitate

CHOOSE for yourselves the ones to imitate, and don't let a little voice say to you: "Where are we to find such people?" Be such people yourselves, and you will find such people.

Like always sticks to like. If you live an abandoned sort of life, only abandoned people will attach themselves to you. Start living a good life, and you'll see how many companions surround you. —*Sermon 228, 2*

PRAYER. *Help me, Lord, to be the sort of person someone else should imitate.* —Sermon 228, 2

APRIL 19
Life in Yourselves

OW that your hearts are sprinkled with a pure conscience and your bodies washed with pure water, "approach Christ and be enlightened and your faces will not blush for shame."

If you receive this worthily, which means belonging to the new covenant by which you hope for an eternal inheritance, and if you keep the new commandment to love one another, then you have life in yourselves.

—*Sermon 228B, 3*

PRAYER. *Let me not be my own life! In You I begin to live again.* —*Confessions XII, 10, 10*

APRIL 20
Lift Up the Heart

THE whole life of real Christians is a matter of "Up with the heart." What does "Up with the heart" mean? Hoping in God, not in yourself. You, after all, are down below, and God is up above; if you put your hope in yourself, your heart is down below—it isn't up above.

That's why, when you hear "Lift up your heart" from the high priest, you answer: "We have lifted it up to the Lord." Try very hard to make your answer a true one. —*Sermon 229, 3*

PRAYER. *O truth-speaking Light, I bring my heart to You lest it beguile me with empty thoughts.* —*Confessions XIII, 6, 7*

APRIL 21
Christ Rose Again; Let Us Live for God

CHRIST suffered; let us die to sin. Christ rose again; let us live for God. Christ passed over from this world to the Father; don't let our hearts stick here below but rather follow to the realms above.

Our Head hung on the tree; let us crucify the lust of the flesh. He lay in the tomb; buried with Him, let us forget the past. He is seated in heaven; let us transfer our desires to sublime realities. —*Sermon 229D, 1*

PRAYER. *Lord, help us to choose our place with good works.* —*Sermon 229D, 1*

APRIL 22
You Can Live, provided You Live

YOU can live, provided you live, that is: you can live forever, provided you live a good life. Don't be afraid of dying a bad death; be afraid indeed, but of living a bad life.

What astonishing perversity! You are all afraid of what none of you can escape, and you don't do what you can certainly do. To avoid dying you can do nothing; to live a good life, this you can do. Do what you can do, and you will have no reason to fear what you can't do.

—*Sermon 229H, 3*

PRAYER. *Lord, You show us what to hope for.*
—*Sermon 229H, 3*

APRIL 23
Take Comfort in the Breaking of the Bread

WHERE did the Lord wish to be recognized [in the Emmaus story]? In the breaking of the bread. We're all right, nothing to worry about; we break bread, and we recognize the Lord.

If you are a believer, any of you, if you are not called a Christian for nothing, if you don't come to church for nothing, if you listen to the word of God in fear and hope, you may take comfort in the breaking of the bread. The Lord's absence is not an absence. Have faith, and the One you cannot see is with you. —*Sermon 235, 3*

PRAYER. *You, Lord, made Yourself present in the breaking of the bread.* —*Sermon 235, 3*

APRIL 24
Life Beyond

I EXHORT and implore you, in the name of the Lord Jesus Christ, through Whom our sins have been forgiven, Who chose that His Blood should be our price, Who saw fit to make us, unfit though we are even to be called His slaves, into His brothers and sisters.

I implore you to direct all your thoughts—that being why you are Christians, why you carry His Name on your foreheads—to nothing but that life we are going to have with the angels where there will be perpetual quiet, everlasting happiness, unfailing bliss, no disturbance, no sadness, no death. *—Sermon 259, 1*

PRAYER. Lord, we carry Your Name on our foreheads. *—Sermon 259, 1*

APRIL 25
It Is God Who Did It

C HRIST rose again; the case is complete and closed. He was body, He was flesh, which hung upon the Cross, gave up the soul, was placed in the tomb. He presented it alive, seeing He lived in it.

Why are we astonished? Why don't we believe? It is God Who did it. Reflect on the One Who brought it about, and you eliminate all possibility of doubt. *—Sermon 242, 1*

PRAYER. May the living live truly, and may the dead endeavor without delay to rise again. *—Sermon 98, 7*

APRIL 26
Let Us Believe about the Head

THE Apostles could see Christ present, but they couldn't see the Church spread throughout the whole world. They could see the Head; they could only believe about the Body.

We have our turn; we have the grace of the times allotted to us in which to believe by God's dispensation. The Apostles could see the Head and could only believe about the Body; we can see the Body; let us believe about the Head.

—*Sermon 242, 12*

PRAYER. *You, O Christ, offered Yourself to their eyes to be seen, but also to their hands to be touched and felt.* —*Sermon 242, 12*

APRIL 27
To Rise Again

GO back to the Word, go back to "In the beginning was the Word, and the Word was with God, and the Word was God," and consider what it means for that One to rise again. Having raised up His own flesh, He will also raise up yours.

The reason, you see, He wished to raise His own again was to preserve you from failing to believe that yours would rise again.

—*Sermon 242A, 1*

PRAYER. *You died, Lord, in the flesh You took, not in the Divinity in which You remained.*

—*Sermon 242A, 1*

APRIL 28
Christ Tore Up the Debtors' Bills

FROM the very beginning, through the man who sinned, we have received this evil inheritance from our father the sinner. But there came to us another inheritance, that of the Man Who took on our inheritance and promised us His own.

We were in possession of death through blame; He took death to Himself without blame. Though He wasn't a debtor, He was put to death, and so tore up the debtors' bills. So, all of you, let your minds be full of faith in the Resurrection. —*Sermon 229H, 1*

PRAYER. Let our minds, O God, be full of faith in the Resurrection. —*Sermon 242A, 3*

APRIL 29
The Distinctive Mark of Our Faith

THE Resurrection of the Lord Jesus Christ is the distinctive mark of the Christian Faith. Many people, both alien to us and godless, have believed that the Lord Christ was born human of a human being.

Although they didn't know that He was born of a virgin, still both friends and enemies have believed that Christ was born a man; both friends and enemies have believed that Christ was crucified and died; but that He rose again, only His friends have known. —*Sermon 229H, 1*

PRAYER. From You, Lord, derives our garment of light. —*Confessions XIII, 8, 9*

APRIL 30
Alleluia!

E are going to come to the house of God in heaven. There we shall praise God, not for fifty days, but, as it is written, "forever and ever."

We shall see, we shall love, we shall praise. Nor shall our seeing come to an end, nor shall our loving fade away, nor shall our praising ever be silent. It will all be everlasting, without end. Let us praise Him, not only with our voices but also with our behavior. —*Sermon 254, 8*

PRAYER. *O my Lord, You will never cease to be the subject of my hymns and praises.*
—*Soliloquies of the Soul with God IV, 3*

MAY 1
The Lord Has Made You

EALIZE that you are "day," realize that the Lord has made you. He has chased away the darkness of sin from your hearts and has made your lives new.

Today you are to be mixed in with the People of God and counted among them. Choose which ones to imitate; don't choose for yourselves abandoned persons with whom to be lost and perish. —*Sermon 260D, 2*

PRAYER. *We are not our own, Lord, but we all belong to You Who shed Your Blood as the price for us.* —*Sermon 260D, 2*

MAY 2
What Is Peace?

WHAT is peace? Listen to the Apostle. He was talking about Christ: "He is our peace Who has made both one." So peace is Christ. Where did it go? "He was crucified and buried, He rose from the dead, He ascended into heaven." There you have where peace went.

"How am I to follow it?" Lift up your heart. Listen to how you should follow: every day you hear it briefly when you are told, "Lift up your heart." *—Sermon 25, 7*

PRAYER. *You are our God Who do not pass away, for there is nothing else to supplant You.* *—Confessions IV, 11, 17*

MAY 3
Alleluia

THE life which is represented by the forty days before Easter is the one we now have; the life which is represented by the fifty days after the Lord's Resurrection is not now being lived, but hoped for, and in being hoped for is loved.

And, by that very love, God Who promised all these things is being praised, and such praises are what "alleluia" is. *—Sermon 243, 8*

PRAYER. *These happy days after the Resurrection stand for the future life, where we will be reigning with You, O Lord.* *—Sermon 243, 8*

MAY 4
Made Into Christ's Brothers and Sisters

LOVE the Lord because He loves you; pay frequent visits to this mother who bore you. Consider what this mother has conferred on you, joining creatures to the Creator, making slaves into children of God, making the devil's henchmen into Christ's brothers and sisters.

You won't show yourselves ungrateful for these immense benefits received from her if you show her the proper consideration of your presence. —*Sermon 255A, 2*

PRAYER. *We cannot hope to have You as a gracious Father, if we neglect the Church as our mother.* —*Sermon 255A, 2*

MAY 5
The Eternal Alleluia of the Blessed

ALLELUIA is praise of God. So the activity of our rest is being indicated to us by it while we are still toiling hard. When we arrive at that rest after this our toil, our only business will be the praise of God—our activity there consists in alleluia. What does alleluia mean? "Praise God." Let us say it as much as we can so that we may deserve to say it always. —*Sermon 252, 9*

PRAYER. *Lord, after this age and after our toil we will find fullness without ceasing in alleluia.* —*Sermon 252, 9*

71

MAY 6
Alleluia in Reality

I T'S in hope that we sing alleluia. Just see what joy there is in hope. What then will the reality itself be like? You want to know what it will be like? Listen to what follows: "They shall get drunk on the plenteousness of Your house." That's the reality hope is about.

We're thirsty, we're hungry; it must be that we shall be satisfied; but hunger while on the road, satisfaction when we get home. When shall we be satisfied? "I shall be satisfied when Your glory is revealed." —*Sermon 231, 2*

PRAYER. *Lord, I shall be satisfied when Your glory is revealed.* —*Sermon 231, 2*

MAY 7
The New Life of Those Who Believe in Jesus

T HE Resurrection of our Lord Jesus Christ is the new life of those who believe in Jesus. And this is the mysterious meaning of His Passion and Resurrection which you certainly ought to know about and live up to.

It was not, after all, without reason that Life came to death, not without reason that "the Fountain of Life," from which one drinks to live, drank here the cup which was not His due. —*Sermon 231, 2*

PRAYER. *You, O Jesus, are the Fountain of Life.* —*Sermon 231, 2*

MAY 8

It Is Foolishness To Assume That Times Past Were Better Than the Present

HAT unusual horror is the human race enduring now, that our ancestors didn't have to endure? Or when do we have to endure such things as we know they endured?

And you'll find people grumbling about their times, and saying that the time of our parents were good. Suppose, though, they could be whisked back to the times of their parents—they would still grumble even then.

—Sermon 346C, 1

PRAYER. *How high and glorious You are, O God, Who make the humble-hearted Your home.* *—Confessions XI, 31, 41*

MAY 9

Faith

EOPLE are told: "Believe," and they want to see. The answer they are given is "In order to see eventually, for the time being believe. Faith does the earning; sight is the reward. If you want to see before you believe, you're demanding to be paid before doing the job.

"What you want has its price. You want to see God; the price of such a tremendous good as that is faith." *—Sermon 359A, 3*

PRAYER. *How high You are in the heights of heaven, how deep in the depths. From no place are You absent.* *—Confessions VIII, 3, 8*

MAY 10

Preaching That a Dead Man Had Risen

NE man [Peter] was dying that Another might be honored, one slain that Another might be worshiped. Would he have done this if he hadn't been on fire with love and utterly convinced of the truth?

The Apostles had seen what they were proclaiming. When would they have been willing to die for something they had not seen? Should they have denied what they had seen? They did not deny it; they preached a dead Man Whom they knew to be alive. —*Sermon 311, 2*

PRAYER. *I come back to You, O God, fevered and panting for Your fountain. Let no one bar my way; let me drink it and draw life from it.*
—*Confessions XII, 10, 10*

MAY 11

The Lord Knows You

E grains of wheat. There are masses of chaff on the threshing floor, but the winnowing is going to come. The chaff will be separated, and not a single wisp of it will enter the granary with you, not a single grain goes on the fire.

The One Who was able to assemble you knows how to separate. You are wrong if you think the Lord can go wrong! —*Sermon 311, 2*

PRAYER. *My good is to hold fast to You, O God.*
—*Confessions VII, 11, 17*

MAY 12
Receive This Rich Guest

IGNORE your own spirit, and receive the Spirit of God. Do not let your spirit be afraid that when the Spirit of God takes up residence in you, your spirit will be squeezed into a corner of your body. When the Spirit of God takes up residence in your body, it won't shut your spirit out; don't worry.

"What am I to do?" you say. "Where am I to go, where am I to move to?" Receive this rich Guest, the Spirit of God. Your space will be widened, not narrowed. —*Sermon 169, 15*

PRAYER. *May we receive the rich Guest, O Lord, and may He not be one of those passing guests.* —*Sermon 169, 15*

MAY 13
Place Your Hope in the Future

WHEN you have been made new, by the forgiveness of your sins, with all your past ones forgiven, if you receive here a long stretch of life, so live that good works follow on your faith. Live up to what you become: a child in the family of so great a Father and Householder, one over whom God's Name is invoked.

Live like that; make progress. Don't bother with the present; place your hope in the future. Let temporal things lose their value for you, and eternal realities grow in importance.

—*Sermon 97A, 4*

PRAYER. *Help us, Lord, to make progress to place our hope in the future.* —*Sermon 97A, 4*

MAY 14
Communion with the Church

ARE you in communion with that Church which is spread through all the nations, beginning from Jerusalem? If you are in communion with it, then you are there, you are in the vine, you haven't been cut off.

It, you see, is the vine which has grown and filled the whole wide world, the Body of Christ, the Church of Christ, whose Head is in heaven.

—Sermon 162A, 10

PRAYER. *O Body of Christ, O holy Church, let all your bones cry, "Lord, who is like You?"*

—On Ps. 34, 14

MAY 15
Let Us All Be Found Together in Christ

BEING lost was the common lot of all of us; let it also be our common lot to be found. We all got lost together; let us all be found together in Christ. What we deserve is very different, but the grace we are offered is the same for us all.

The grace of God wipes out what you have contracted; it wipes out too what you have added. "For where sin abounded, grace abounded all the more." *—Sermon 115, 4*

PRAYER. *May we be found in You, Lord, for in ourselves we were lost.*

—The Lord's Sermon on the Mount 55, 3

MAY 16

He Is Not Absent If He Is Held in the Heart

IF Christ were to be presented to us now, and stand right here before us, and say nothing, how would we know Who He was? If He said nothing, what good would that be for us? Isn't it better for Him to speak in the Gospel, though absent, than to be present and say nothing?

And yet He isn't absent if He's held in the heart. Believe in Him, and you see Him. He isn't in front of your eyes; He is in possession of your heart. —*Sermon 263, 3*

PRAYER. *How great is Your glory, O Christ, as You ascend into heaven.* —*Sermon 263, 3*

MAY 17

O Blissful Alleluia!

BLISSFUL alleluia in heaven where the angels are God's temple! There supreme harmony reigns among those who are praising because there is no anxiety about their exultant singing. That is because there is no "law in the members fighting against the law of the mind," no aggressive cupidity there, to endanger the victory of charity.

So here let us sing alleluia while still anxious and worrying so that there we may be able to sing it one day without any worry or care.

—*Sermon 256, 1*

PRAYER. *Let us praise the Lord with our lives and our tongues.* —*Sermon 256, 1*

MAY 18

Faith Is the Conviction of Things Unseen

LOVE kindles hope, and hope shines through love. But when we attain to the things we have been hoping for while believing in and not seeing them, what faith will there be then to be praised?

Considering that "faith is the conviction of things which cannot be seen," when we do see it won't be called faith. After all, you will be seeing, not believing. —*Sermon 359A, 5*

PRAYER. *When we finally arrive to You, O Lord, we are finished with faith, finished with hope.* —*Sermon 256, 1*

MAY 19

Let Christ Wake Up and Talk to You

WHEN does Christ go to sleep in your heart, if not when you forget your faith? Faith in Christ in your heart is like Christ in the boat. You hear nasty stories about yourself, you lose heart, you get upset. Christ is asleep.

Wake Christ up, wake up your faith. You have something you can do even when you are upset; stir up your faith. Let Christ wake up and talk to you. —*Sermon 163B, 6*

PRAYER. *Believe what is said, and a great calm will settle in your heart.* —*Sermon 163B, 6*

MAY 20
Christ Took a Human Form

THE Lord Jesus, the only-begotten Son of the Father, and co-eternal with His Begetter, equally invisible, equally unchanging, equally omnipotent, equally God, became Man, as you know, as you have received, as you firmly believe, for our sakes taking a human form without losing the Divine, His power hidden, His weakness manifest.

He was born that we might be born again; He died that we might not die forever.—*Sermon 262, 1*

PRAYER. *You, O Christ, offered Yourself to their eyes to be seen, but also to their hands to be touched and felt.* —*Sermon 242, 12*

MAY 21
God Will Make a Way Out

YOU have entered into temptation, but God will also make a way out so that you do not perish in the temptation; so that, like a potter's jar, you may be shaped by the preaching, cooked by the tribulation.

But when you enter the temptation, bear in mind the way out; because God is faithful, "God will watch over your going in and your coming out." —*Sermon 256, 3*

PRAYER. *Among the trials and temptations of this life, both by others and by us let alleluia be sung.* —*Sermon 256, 3*

MAY 22
Love Peace

LOVE peace, and pray to the Lord for peace. So let peace be our beloved and our mistress, and our hearts be the chaste couch we share with her.

It's harder to praise peace than to possess her. If we wish to praise her, we have to rally our powers, put our ideas together, weigh our words; but if we wish to possess her, we can do so without the slightest effort. —*Sermon 357, 1*

PRAYER. *You have taught us, Lord: the true lover of peace also loves His enemies.*

—*Sermon 357, 1*

MAY 23
We Are Sighing in This Life for Our True Country

IN this life we are still wandering exiles, still sighing in faith for I know not what kind of home country. And why "I know not what kind," seeing that we are its citizens, unless it is because by wandering away "into a far country" we have forgotten our true native land?

This amnesia is driven from our hearts by the Lord Christ, King of that country, as He comes to join us in our exile; and by His taking of flesh, His Divinity becomes a way for us, so that we may proceed along it through Christ as Man, and abide in Christ as God. —*Sermon 362, 4*

PRAYER. *In You, Lord, we walk together by faith, not yet by sight.* —*Sermon 362, 4*

MAY 24
He Will Come Openly

THE glorification of our Lord Jesus Christ was completed by His rising again and ascending into heaven. The reason He rose again was to show us an example of resurrection, and the reason He ascended was to protect us from above.

So we have our Lord and Savior Jesus Christ first hanging on the tree, now seated in heaven. He paid our price when He was hanging on the tree; He has been gathering up what He bought while seated in heaven.

—Sermon 263, 1

PRAYER. *You will come openly, Lord, in order to judge.* *—Sermon 263, 1*

MAY 25
Grace Given Gratis

IF you are relying on your works, it follows that you are being paid a reward, not presented with a grace. But if it is a grace, then it is given gratis, free.

Now I'm going to question you: Do you believe Christ, you sinner? You say, "I do." What do you believe? That all your sins can be forgiven you through Him gratis? You already have what you believe. Oh, grace given gratis!

—Sermon 100, 4

PRAYER. *In Your loving kindness we are just; in our iniquity we are sinners.* *—Sermon 100, 4*

MAY 26

We Must Hurry to Jerusalem

THERE is a Jerusalem which the Apostle says is in heaven; yes, there is a Jerusalem above which "is the mother of us all." He calls her a mother, like a metropolis; metropolis, you see, means "mother city."

So that is the one to which we must be hurrying along, knowing that we are still away abroad and are on the way. *—Sermon 346B, 1*

PRAYER. *Let me sing my songs of love to You, giving vent to my inarticulate groans as I walk my pilgrim way, remembering Jerusalem and lifting up my heart toward her.*

—Confessions XII, 16, 23

MAY 27

Show Mercy in Order To Receive Mercy

THERE is always a medicine available to be applied to what are practically daily wounds; the medicine consists of good works of mercy.

I mean, if you want to obtain God's mercy, be merciful yourself. If you refuse to show humanity to a human being, though human yourself, God will refuse you Divinity: that is to say, the imperishable immortality by which He makes us gods. *—Sermon 259, 3*

PRAYER. *Let mercy triumph over judgment, for You, Whose utterances are true, have to the merciful promised mercy.* *—Confessions IX, 13, 35*

MAY 28
One Love, One Spirit

NE love and two commandments; one Spirit and two givings. It wasn't one given first and another given later; because it is not a different love which loves the neighbor from the one which loves God. So it's not another love.

With the same love as we love our neighbor, let us also love God. But because God is one thing and our neighbor another, they are loved with one love, and yet they are not one thing being loved. —*Sermon 265, 9*

PRAYER. *Let all of us love one another and likewise love You, our God, the Fount of Truth.* —*Confessions XII, 30, 41*

MAY 29
Do Not Yet Consider Yourself Safe

HOSE who don't yet keep to the right road are caught in the greater danger; but as for those who are already on the highway, yes, they too should not consider themselves safe.

For they may be held back by the delights of the road itself, and not be drawn on by as much love as they should be to that home country where alone true rest is to be found. —*Sermon 346B, 2*

PRAYER. *If we love, we are running; and the more consistently we love, the faster we run.* —*Sermon 346B, 2*

MAY 30
May We Touch Him in Faith

MAY Christ ascend for us, and may we touch Him, which we will do if we believe in Him: that He is the Son of God, eternal, co-eternal, not from the time He was born of the virgin, but eternal. Us too, after all, He is going to make eternal.

Believe like that, and you have touched. Touch like that in order to cling to Him. Cling like that, so as never to be separated from Him but to continue with Him in the greatness of His Divinity, Who died for us in the weakness of His Humanity. —*Sermon 229L, 2*

PRAYER. *Lord, may we touch You in faith.*

—*Sermon 229L, 2*

MAY 31
God Is the Life of the Living

THROUGH the form of a servant the Creator of things visible and invisible "ascended into heaven" from where He had never departed; through this form of a servant "He is seated at the right hand of the Father" Whose arm He is.

In this form of a servant He is going to come to judge the living and the dead, the form which He chose to share with the dead, though He is the life of the living. —*Sermon 212, 1*

PRAYER. *You, O Christ, emptied Yourself, not losing the form of God but taking the form of a servant.*

—*Sermon 212, 1*

JUNE 1
You Are God's Praise

YOU do want to sing about the One you love. You are asking for praises of His to sing. You have been told: "Sing to the Lord a new song." You are looking for praise songs, are you? "His praise is the Church of the saints." The praise of the One to be sung about are those who sing.

Do you want to sing the praises of God? Be yourselves what you sing. You are God's praise if you lead good lives. —*Sermon 34, 6*

PRAYER. *May my heart and my tongue give praise to You.* —*Confessions IX, 1, 1*

JUNE 2
Be a Part of Him

IF no one has gone up except the One Who has come down, and He is the Son of Man, our Lord Jesus, do you too want to go up? Be a part of Him, with the rest of His Body, Who is the only one to go up.

He, the Head, is one person, one man. And since none can go up unless they have been incorporated in Him as members of His Body, this text is verified, that "No one has gone up into heaven except Him Who came down."

—*Sermon 91, 7*

PRAYER. *By Your fire, Your beneficent fire, we are enflamed, because we are making our way up.* —*Confessions XIII, 9, 10*

JUNE 3

Who Wouldn't Want To Follow Christ?

HEAVEN was a long, long way away from us before our Head had gone up to heaven. Now, though, what reason have we to despair if we are the Body and limbs of that Head? So that's where we have to follow Him.

Who wouldn't want to follow Him to such a residence? Who wouldn't want to follow Christ there where total happiness reigns? —*Sermon 96, 3*

PRAYER. *Stand still, O Light; enlighten my eyes that they may receive some brightness from Your wonderful light which You reveal in heaven.*
—*Soliloquies of the Soul with God II, 4*

JUNE 4

The Miracle of the Whole World Believing

THOUGH containing all things, Jesus was conceived; though giving birth to all things, He was born; though giving life to all things, He died; but after three days He rose again and ascended into heaven and placed the human flesh He had taken to Himself at the Father's right hand.

It's a miracle that a Man should have risen again in the flesh, but it's a much greater miracle that the whole world should have believed something so unbelievable. —*Sermon 272 A*

PRAYER. *O Lord, You help the downtrodden to their feet, and they do not fall, for their high dignity is Yourself.* —*Confessions XI, 31, 41*

JUNE 5

One Loaf, One Body, Many Though We Be

THE bread which you can see on the altar, sanctified by the word of God, is the Body of Christ. That cup, or rather what the cup contains, sanctified by the word of God, is the Blood of Christ. It was by means of these things that the Lord Christ willed to present us with His Body and Blood, which He shed for our sake for the forgiveness of sins.

If you receive them well, you are yourselves what you receive: one Loaf, one Body, many though we be. —*Sermon 227*

PRAYER. *You, Lord, made Yourself present in the breaking of the bread.* —*Sermon 235, 3*

JUNE 6

Dust from Dust in Dust

A POOR man might say to you: "Why are you being so conceited? Because you've given me, a poor beggar, something? Some bread. If you put this bread aside in your house and forgot about it, it would grow moldy, get worm-eaten, and turn into dust; dust would revert to dust.

"You, indeed, when my hand was stretched out to receive, have stretched your hand out to give; but remember what your hand was made from, and what you have placed in mine: dust from dust in dust." —*Sermon 389, 3*

PRAYER. *Help us to know what we are giving but also what we are receiving.* —*Sermon 389, 3*

JUNE 7
Lift Up Your Hearts

THERE are faithful human beings, already distinguished in heart from the mass of unbelievers, always looking to God, those who are told: "Lift up your hearts," who cherish an altogether different hope and who know that they are "aliens and exiles" in this world.

They occupy the middle ground; they are to be compared neither with those people who think the only good is to enjoy earthly delights nor yet awhile with those sublime inhabitants of heaven whose whole delight is in the Bread by which they were created. —*Sermon 400, 2*

PRAYER. *Lord, we must change our heart, lift up our heart, and not allow our heart to make its home here.* —*On Ps. 39, 28*

JUNE 8
Thanks Be to God

THERE are just two sayings: God and neighbor; the One Who made you and the one He made you with. No one has told you: "Love the sun, love the moon, love the earth and everything that has been made."

These are the things in which God is to be praised, the Maker to be blessed. —*Sermon 16A, 6*

PRAYER. *We have sinned, and we have been sought. Thanks be to You!* —*Sermon 16A, 6*

JUNE 9
Give Us Bread

THE Lord says: "I received bread; I will give bread. I received drink; I will give a drink. I received hospitality; I will give a home. I was visited in sickness; I will give health. I was visited in prison; I will give freedom.

"The bread which you gave to My poor has been eaten up; the Bread which I will give both fills and never fails." —*Sermon 86, 5*

PRAYER. *May You, Lord, give us Bread, You being the Bread which came down from heaven.* —*Sermon 84, 5*

JUNE 10
A Food That Appeals to Everyone

IF you are seeking food because you have been fasting, "blessed are those who hunger and thirst for justice." But it is said of the Lord Jesus Christ Himself that He has become for us justice and wisdom. There you have the banquet that has been provided.

Christ is justice; nowhere is He in short supply; He is not provided for us by cooks nor is He imported by merchants from overseas like exotic fruits. He is a Food that appeals to everyone. —*Sermon 28, 2*

PRAYER. *You, Lord, are light and voice, and fragrance for our hearts.* —*Sermon 28, 2*

89

JUNE 11
Be Mindful of This Grace

CHRIST our Lord, Who offered by suffering for us what by being born He had received from us, has become our high priest forever and has given us the order of sacrifice which you can see, of His Body, that is to say, and His Blood. When His Body, you remember, was pierced by the lance, it poured forth the water and the Blood by which He canceled our sins.

Be mindful of the grace as you work out your salvation, since it is God Who is at work in you, and approach with fear and trembling to partake of this altar. —*Sermon 228B, 2*

PRAYER. *Lord, may we recognize in the Bread what hung on the Cross, and in the Cup what flowed from Your side.* —*Sermon 228B, 2*

JUNE 12
The Wedding Garment

EXPLAIN the wedding garment to us, you will say. There is no doubt at all that it is a garment which only the good have, those who are to be left at the banquet, preserved for the banquet to which no bad person has access, to be brought through to it by the grace of the Lord.

These are the ones who have on the wedding garment. —*Sermon 90, 5-6*

PRAYER. *Teach us, Lord, that the wedding garment is love from a pure heart.* —*Sermon 90, 5*

JUNE 13
Have Faith Together with Love

AVE faith together with love, because you can't have love without faith. I'm not urging you to have faith, but love. Because you can't have love without faith; I mean, of course, love of God and neighbor.

How can these exist without faith? How can you love God if you don't believe in God?

—*Sermon 90, 8*

PRAYER. *Give me, O Lord, a deep understanding of Your wisdom so that my love may be ardent, faithful, and ever unchanging.*

—*Soliloquies I, 11*

JUNE 14
Doing Things for One Another

OME people have plenty of money. Let them feed the poor, clothe the naked, build a church, and use their money for whatever good purposes they can. Other people have the gift of counsel. Let them guide their neighbors, dispersing the darkness of doubt with the light of loving faith.

Still others have the ability to teach. Let them make distribution from the storerooms of the Lord, handing out food to their fellow servants, confirming the faithful, calling back those who stray, seeking the lost, as best they can.

—*Sermon 91, 9*

PRAYER. *May we bear one another's burdens and accomplish the law of Christ.* —*Sermon 91, 9*

JUNE 15

You Were Made into the Lord's Loaf of Bread

 REMEMBER, you didn't exist; then you were created, carried to the Lord's threshing floor, and threshed by the labor of the oxen, that is, of the preachers of the Gospel.

When, as catechumens, you were being held back, you were being stored in the barn. You gave in your names; then you began to be ground by fasts and exorcisms. Afterward you came to the water, were moistened into dough, and made into one lump. With the heat of the Holy Spirit you were baked and made into the Lord's loaf of bread. —*Sermon 229, 1*

PRAYER. *The bread and wine, when the word is applied to it, becomes the Body and Blood of Your Son, O God.* —*Sermon 229, 1*

JUNE 16

Pardon Is Given by the Forgiver of Sins

 THE best of doctors has begun to cure you, and for Him no disease is incurable. Don't be afraid for your past wickedness, however frightful, however unbelievable. They are grave diseases, but the Doctor has mastered them.

So don't worry about past sins; in one moment of the Sacrament they will be forgiven, and absolutely all of them will be totally forgiven. —*Sermon 97A, 2*

PRAYER. *You, Lord, the Forgiver of sins, grant us pardon.* —*Sermon 97A, 2*

JUNE 17
I Was a Stranger, and You Took Me In

LEARN to take in strangers as guests where Christ can be recognized. Or didn't you know that if you take in any Christian, you are taking Him in? Didn't He say Himself: "I was a stranger, and you took Me in"?

And when He's asked: "Lord, when did we see You a stranger?" He answers: "When you did it to one of the least of Mine you did it to Me." So when a Christian takes in a Christian, members are serving members. —*Sermon 236, 3*

PRAYER. *You, Lord, are recognized in the breaking of the bread.* —*Sermon 236, 3*

JUNE 18
Released from the Big Squeeze

YOU cannot live good lives unless Truth helps you to, unless He gives you the power, unless He grants it to you. Pray for that and eat. Pray, and you will be released from that squeeze because He will fill you, both in doing good and in living good lives.

Let your consciences be closely inspected. Then your mouths will be filled with the praise of God and rejoicing, and you will be released from the big squeeze and tremendous pressure. —*Sermon 132A, 2*

PRAYER. *May our mouths be filled with praise of You, O God.* —*Sermon 236, 3*

JUNE 19
Faith Is a Gift of God

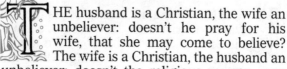THE husband is a Christian, the wife an unbeliever: doesn't he pray for his wife, that she may come to believe? The wife is a Christian, the husband an unbeliever: doesn't the religious woman pray for her husband, that he may come to believe?

What are they praying for but that God would give that person faith! So faith is a gift of God. —*Sermon 168, 8*

PRAYER. *You, O Lord, show Yourself to any-one who loves You according to Your bidding.*
—*Confessions XII, 15, 19*

JUNE 20
What You Don't See Now, Believe

WHAT you can see passes away, yet the invisible reality signified does not pass away, but remains. Is the Body of Christ consumed, is the Church of Christ consumed, are the members of Christ consumed? Perish the thought! Here they are being purified; there they will be crowned with the victor's laurels.

What is signified will remain eternally even though the thing that signifies it seems to pass away. So receive the Sacrament in such a way that you think about yourselves, that you retain unity in your hearts, that you always fix your hearts up above. —*Sermon 227*

PRAYER. *Let not our hope, Lord, be placed on earth, but in heaven.* —*Sermon 227*

JUNE 21
Children of God

LOVE what you will be. What you will be, you see, is children of God and sons and daughters by adoption. This will be given you free, conferred on you for nothing, at His pleasure.

In this you will be the more abundantly and richly and plentifully endowed, the more pleasing you are to the One from Whom you have received all this. —*Sermon 216, 8*

PRAYER. *If you lift yourself high, God will withdraw far away from you; if you humble yourself, God will come near to you.*

—*On Ps. 50, 21*

JUNE 22
Kindness

KINDNESS is what you must practice because sins abound. There is no other relief, no other road by which we can reach God, by which we can be made whole, be reconciled to Him Whom we have so dangerously offended.

We are going to come into His presence: may our works speak up for us there—and so speak up that they outweigh our offenses. It's the side that's heavier that will gain the day, either for punishment if our sins deserve it, or for relief and rest if our good works do. —*Sermon 259, 4*

PRAYER. *In our hearts, Lord, we display what we are before You.* —*Sermon 259, 4*

JUNE 23
Tread the Mountaintops

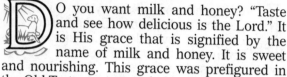

O you want milk and honey? "Taste and see how delicious is the Lord." It is His grace that is signified by the name of milk and honey. It is sweet and nourishing. This grace was prefigured in the Old Testament, revealed in the New.

Whoever worships God in the New Testament should be hoping for the new inheritance, not the old one. If you are hoping for the new inheritance, go beyond the earth, tread the mountaintops, that is to say: despise the lofty station of the proud. —*Sermon 25, 2*

PRAYER. *If we have lifted up our heart to You, Lord, then You hold our heart to stop it from falling to the earth.* —*Sermon 25, 2*

JUNE 24
Let Us Imitate John the Baptist

IMPLY as human beings let us humble ourselves, and not boast except in the Lord, that He may be exalted; let us, in ourselves, diminish, so that in Him we may grow.

Consider John the Baptist, that greatest of men, than whom among those born of women nobody has arisen greater; what did he say about Christ, "He must grow; I, however, must diminish." Let God grow, and humans diminish. —*Sermon 293D, 5*

PRAYER. *Whatever we are that is good, we attribute to You, O Good God.* —*Sermon 293D, 5*

JUNE 25
The Inner Eye

GOD made you to His image. Do you think He would give you the wherewithal to see the sunlight which He made and not give you the wherewithal to see the One Who made you, considering that He made you to His own image?

Of course, He gave this too: He gave you both capacities. But you are greatly attached to these outer eyes and thoroughly negligent of the inner eye—you carry it around all worn out and damaged. —*Sermon 88, 6*

PRAYER. *With Your help I will understand, when You grant me this gift, O gracious Light of my secret eyes.* —*Confessions XI, 19, 25*

JUNE 26
They Preach Peace, and They Have Peace

SUCH should Christ's apostles be, preachers of the Gospel, not greeting on the road; that is, not looking for something else, but proclaiming the Gospel out of genuine brotherly love, let them come to the house and say, "Peace be to this house." They don't only say it with their lips; they pour out what they are full of. They preach peace, and they have peace. —*Sermon 101, 11*

PRAYER. *Needy and poor am I, but I am the better for recognizing it and lamenting it in secret and seeking Your mercy until my imperfect self is brought to perfection in peace.*

—*Confessions. X, 38, 63*

JUNE 27
Spending Money on the Poor

 NOBODY should be afraid of spending money on the poor. Nobody should imagine that the One Who receives it is the one whose outstretched hand he sees. The one who receives it is the One Who ordered you to give it.

And this isn't just my own idea; I'm not saying it as a piece of merely human guesswork: listen to Him as He both gives you a warning and writes you out a guarantee. "I was hungry," He says, "and you gave Me to eat." —*Sermon 86, 3*

PRAYER. *I cry out to You in a frame of mind that understands my need. I cry to You in the knowledge that I will always be a pauper as long as I do not possess You Who make me rich.*

—On Ps. 33, II, 11

JUNE 28
God Seeks His Image in Your Character

JUST as Caesar seeks his image in your coin, so God seeks His image in your character. "Give back to Caesar," He says, "what belongs to Caesar."

What does Caesar look for from you? His image. What does God look for from you? His image. But Caesar's image is on a coin; God's image is in you. —*Sermon 113A, 8*

PRAYER. *O loving Physician, wash my soul in the waters of tribulation so that, shining like a mirror, it may receive the imprint of Your image.* —*Soliloquies of the Soul with God II, 10*

JUNE 29
"I Will Lay Down My Life for You"

BLESSED Peter, the first of the Apostles, both lover and repudiator of the Lord Jesus Christ, followed the Lord as He was about to suffer; but at that time he was not able to follow Him to the extent of suffering himself. He followed with his feet; he wasn't yet capable of following with his virtue. He promised he would die *for* Him, and he wasn't even able to die *with* Him.

He had promised more than he could fulfill because it was in fact unfitting that he should do what he had promised: "I will lay down my life for You." —*Sermon 296, 1*

PRAYER. Lord, grant us the strength so to love You that we are capable of also dying for You. —*Sermon 296, 1*

JUNE 30
Exult and Rejoice

EXULT and rejoice on the days of the holy martyrs; pray that you may be able to follow in the footsteps of the martyrs.

It isn't, after all, that you are human beings and they weren't; not the case that you were born and they were born quite differently. We are all from Adam; we are all trying to be in Christ. —*Sermon 273, 9*

PRAYER. As for those who feed on Your truth in the wide pastures of charity, let me be united with them in You. —*Confessions XII, 23, 32*

JULY 1
Death Cannot Be Eliminated

THE loss of our dear ones is something we fear: it's possible we may lose them and possible we won't. Whatever bad thing you may fear on this earth, it may possibly happen and may possibly not.

However, death cannot possibly not happen. It can be delayed; it can't be eliminated. And yet everybody works so hard to put off the evil day! This, too, then is to be counted among the things to be put up with and endured patiently: the fear of death. —*Sermon 359A, 8*

PRAYER. *From no place are You absent, Lord, yet how tardily do we return to You.*

—*Confessions VIII, 3, 8*

JULY 2
Ask, and You Will Receive

LET us all, human as we are, examine ourselves; and whatever good we find in ourselves that concerns our justification, let us give thanks for it to the One Who gave it to us. And in giving thanks to the One Who gave it to us, let us also ask Him for what He has not yet given us.

Don't imagine, I mean, that you profit by receiving and He loses by giving. However capacious the gullet, however capacious the belly you bring, the Fountain infinitely surpasses your thirst. —*Sermon 159, 9*

PRAYER. *My faith calls upon You, Lord, this faith which is Your gift to me.* —*Confessions I, 1, 1*

JULY 3
We Know by Faith

ET your feet firmly on the way; set them there so that you don't leave the way, not so that you stick on the way, but, as it is written, "so run that you may attain." Let Christ flourish always in your hearts, the Christ Who wished to show in the Head what the other members should hope for.

We indeed are toiling away on earth; our Head in heaven now neither dies nor fails in any way nor suffers anything at all. He did, all the same, suffer for us. We know this by faith, while those He showed Himself to learned it by their eyes. *—Sermon 361, 13*

PRAYER. *Because of our sins we are in darkness; but You, my God, will illuminate my darkness.* *—On Ps. 17, 29*

JULY 4
Hungry and Thirsty for Justice

AUL, hungry and thirsty for justice, says he is not yet perfect because he has not yet received, not yet attained; he says he is stretching out, says he is following on to the palm of the calling from above.

He is on the way; he's hungry, he wants to be filled, he's busy about it, he longs to arrive, he's simmering with impatience—nothing seems to him to be so long delayed as his "casting off and being with Christ." *—Sermon 400, 1*

PRAYER. *Help us, Lord, to keep on walking to forge ahead.* *—Sermon 169, 18*

JULY 5
Deliver Us from Evil

TOLERANCE is absolutely necessary in this life for the poor, the rich, the healthy, the sick, for captives, for free persons, for exiles, for foreigners, for those settled in their own country; tolerance is necessary because all alike are exiles and foreigners in the world.

And until they are delivered from this exile, and are united to that Truth, to that Unchanging Reality for which they have been sighing, they are beset with trial and temptations, and cry to God, "Deliver us from evil." —*Sermon 359A, 5*

PRAYER. *Lord, give me the insight to understand that justice, of which good and holy people are the servants.* —*Confessions III, 7, 14*

JULY 6
Christ Became Our Fellow Citizen

WE didn't know the way, and the Chief Citizen of this city made Himself into the way. The road had many twists and turns, thorny and stony and extremely difficult.

The Leader Himself, Who is the Prince there, came down here. He came down to seek out the citizens of that city. We had all gone astray. He came down here looking for us citizens, and He became our fellow citizen. —*Sermon 16A, 9*

PRAYER. *O God, You sent Your Son that by His example we might learn even a humility like His.* —*Confessions X, 43, 68*

JULY 7

The Right Order of Love

WHATEVER you love to the neglect of God, it was God Who made it. Because if it wasn't beautiful, it wouldn't be valued by you; and where could its beauty come from if it were not created by the One Who is invisible, beautiful?

I don't want you doing no loving at all, but I want your loving to be rightly ordered. Put heavenly things before earthly ones. Put the Lord before everything else, not just for praising but for loving. —*Sermon 335C, 13*

PRAYER. *You, Lord, made heaven and earth. You are beautiful and they are beautiful, yet not the way You are beautiful.* —*Confessions XI, 4, 6*

JULY 8

Count Yourselves Fortunate

THE times in the past you think were good were only good for the simple reason that they weren't your times. It was Adam who was told, "In the sweat of your face shall you eat your bread, and you shall work the ground." That's what he deserved, and that's what he received from the last judgment of God.

So why do you think that times past were better than your times? We have more reason to count ourselves fortunate than to grumble about our times. —*Sermon 346C, 1*

PRAYER. *Lord, let us love You and run to You.*
—*Confessions VIII, 4, 9*

JULY 9

It Is Something Great To Live a Blessed Life

HERE'S nothing great about living a long time, or even living forever; but it is something great to live a blessed life.

Let us love eternal life and gauge how hard we ought to strive for it from the way in which we see people who love this temporal life that is bound to end sometime strive so hard for it, that when the fear of death looms up they do everything they can, not to eliminate death, but simply to put it off. —*Sermon 127, 2*

PRAYER. *Let my prayer reach You. My longing for the joys You will lavish upon us in eternity has wrung this prayer from me and launched it on its way to You.* —*On Ps. 53, 5*

JULY 10

Let Us Love God

OVE Christ; long for the Light which Christ is. If the blind man longed for the light of the body, how much more ought you all to long for the Light of the heart?

Let us cry out to Him with our behavior. Let us lead good lives; let everything that passes away be as nothing. —*Sermon 349, 5*

PRAYER. *O Justice and Innocence, fair and lovely, it is on You that I want to gaze with eyes that see purely and find satiety in never being sated.* —*Confessions II, 10, 18*

JULY 11
He Has Bestowed Hope on Our Flesh

THE Lord Jesus Christ has through His Flesh bestowed hope on our flesh. He took to Himself what we know all about on this earth, what there was plenty of here: being born and dying. As for rising again and living forever, there was none of that here.

He found here the cheap merchandise of earth; He brought with Him the exotic wares of heaven. If the prospect of death alarms you, be attracted by that of the resurrection.

—Sermon 124, 4

PRAYER. *On the Cross, Lord, You demonstrate the downfall of our old self.* *—Sermon 231, 2*

JULY 12
Leave All to Your God

YOUR little son is crying for you to lift him onto a horse. So you listen; do you let him have his way? Are you being cruel or in fact kind? Ask yourself if your Lord is perhaps dealing with you in the same way when you ask for unsuitable things and you don't get them.

Perhaps want may instruct you, plenty corrupt you. You are asking for the plenty of corruption when what you need, maybe, is the want, the neediness of instruction. Leave it to your God, Who knows what to give you and what to take away from you. *—Sermon 21, 8*

PRAYER. *My eyes are fixed on Your mercy, Lord.* *—Confessions X, 34, 53*

JULY 13
Inner Wealth

YOU who are poor, don't despise your-selves. There is nothing so rich as faith. Your outer storeroom is empty, but your inner coffers are full. Full coffers are a good conscience.

Everything Job possessed outwardly the holy man had taken away from him by the devil. But the inner coffers the devil did not get at. With these Job was rich, so that he could say: "The Lord gave, the Lord has taken away."
—*Sermon 25A, 3*

PRAYER. *As it pleases the Lord, so may it happen. Blessed be the Name of the Lord!*
—*Sermon 25A, 3*

JULY 14
Hold God Fast as Your Good

THIS is the first commandment, this is the beginning of our religion and our journey and road—to have our hearts fixed firmly in faith, and by fixing our hearts firmly in faith to live good lives, to abstain from seductive goods, to endure pa-tiently temporal evils, and as long as the en-ticement of the first and the second persist, to keep our hearts steady and unshaken against each of them.

In doing so, you shall hold God fast as your good and have no evil to endure. —*Sermon 38, 5*

PRAYER. *You go on carrying me, Lord, until Your work is finished in me.* —*On Ps. 85, 7*

JULY 15
He Paid Us His Death in Advance

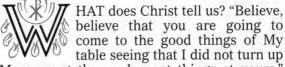 HAT does Christ tell us? "Believe, believe that you are going to come to the good things of My table seeing that I did not turn up My nose at the unpleasant things at yours." So He took your bad things and will give you His good things? Yes, of course He will.

He promised us His life, but what He actually did is even more unbelievable: He paid us His death in advance. —*Sermon 231, 5*

PRAYER. *You are our God Who do not pass away, for there is nothing else to supplant You.* —*Confessions IV, 11, 17*

JULY 16
Give to the Lord from What Is His Own

ISTEN to me, Mr. Rich Man, and let my advice win your approval. Redeem your sins with almsgiving. Don't sit on your gold like a hen on her eggs.

Naked you came from your mother's womb, and naked you are going to return into the earth. And if you are going to return naked into the earth, for whom are you amassing all these things upon the earth? —*Sermon 350B*

PRAYER. *In our hearts, Lord, we display what we are before You.* —*Sermon 259, 4*

JULY 17
The Heavenly Bank

THOSE who are trustworthy put their trust in the power of their Lord. They trust Him to keep their deposit, and they find what He keeps for them. After all, even people who deposit money don't see the vault, do they, or the money in the vault?

They keep on saving and depositing it, or else they dig a hole and keep it there. They don't see it, and yet they have a kind of easy conscience about it because they know it's there in the place they put it. —*Sermon 18, 3*

PRAYER. *When we put our deposit of works of mercy in Your heavenly bank, O Lord, we are sure about Your keeping it safe.*

—*Sermon 18, 3*

JULY 18
In You My Soul Puts Its Trust

THERE remains only one thing we are really free to say: " 'Have mercy on me.' As for any merits of mine to oblige you to have mercy on me, what can I put on the list?

"Not my just deeds, not my riches, not my strength. Not then because of my merits but because 'in You my soul puts its trust.' "

—*Sermon 20A, 2*

PRAYER. *O Lord, You help the downtrodden to their feet, and they do not fall, for their high dignity is Yourself.* —*Confessions XI, 31, 41*

JULY 19

Attend to the Poor, and Do Good Works

TTEND to the poor, whether they are lying on the ground or whether they are walking about; attend to the poor, and do good works. If you are in the habit of doing so, do so; if you are not in the habit of doing so, do so. Let there be an increase in the number of do-gooders because there is an increase, certainly, in the number of the faithful.

When you do something, you can't yet see the quantity of the good you do, just as when the countryman sows he can't yet see the crop, but he trusts the earth. You, then, why don't you trust God? —*Sermon 102, 5*

PRAYER. *I put my trust in You, O Lord.*
—*Sermon 102, 5*

JULY 20

You Are Giving to Christ When You Give to a Needy Person

OU are giving to Christ when you give to a needy person—or are you afraid that such a keeper may lose some of what you give, or that such a rich person may not be able to pay you back?

God is almighty, Christ is almighty; you can't possibly lose any of it. When do you entrust it to Him? When you give to the poor. Such riches don't pass away. —*Sermon 113B, 4*

PRAYER. *You, Lord, wished to bring support from heaven to all who labor.* —*Sermon 113B, 4*

JULY 21
The Property Which Is Peace Grows Bigger

LOVE peace, have peace, be in possession of peace, and take to yourself as many others as you can to be in possession of peace with you.

The more people it is possessed by the more extensive it will be. An earthly house hasn't got room for many; the property which is peace grows even bigger the more inhabitants it has.
—Sermon 357, 1

PRAYER. *You touched me, and I burned for Your peace.* *—Confessions X, 27, 38*

JULY 22
The Real Thing

BEFORE the real thing comes to us, before we come to the real thing, let us take delight in the Lord. It's no trifling delight that is to be had in hope of the real thing that is coming later. Even in these temporal things, in the delights of the world, not the Lord, many people love all sorts of things and haven't yet got the things they love.

So now love in hope. That's why the psalmist says, "The just man takes delight in the Lord." And straightaway, because he does not yet see Him, he adds, "and will hope in Him."

—Sermon 21, 1

PRAYER. *We love You, Lord, in hope.*

—Sermon 21, 1

JULY 23

Give from What You Have in Order To Receive from What You Don't Have

GIVE to the person who doesn't have something because there is something you too don't have. So give from what you have in order to receive from what you don't have.

Let the beggar hammer at your door while you for your part hammer at the door of the Lord. God treats His beggar as you treat yours. So "give, and you will be given"; but if you're unwilling to, look out for yourself. —*Sermon 350B*

PRAYER. *Lord, help us to give from what we have in order to receive from what we do not have.* —*Sermon 350B*

JULY 24

Love Is the Hand of the Soul

THINK of ordinary human love; think of it as the hand of the soul. If it's holding one thing, it can't hold another. To be able to hold something it's given, it must let go of what it's already holding.

What I'm saying is, and mark that I'm saying it plainly: if you love the world, you cannot love God; you've got your hand full. —*Sermon 125, 7*

PRAYER. *Don't let what we possess in this world grip our hand which should be gripping You, O God.* —*Sermon 125, 7*

JULY 25
Transfer Your Wealth to Heaven

WHATEVER it is you love, you have it here on earth; you have what you love in a place where you can lose it and be lost yourself. My advice to you is: transfer it to heaven.

If you keep it here, you will lose what you have, and you will perish together with what you lose; but if you keep it there, you haven't lost it but will yourself follow what you have sent ahead. —*Sermon 389, 4*

PRAYER. *Blessed is the one who loves You, Lord, and loves his friend in You and his enemy for Your sake.* —*Confessions IV, 9, 14*

JULY 26
Three Kinds of Life in the Church

THERE are three kinds of life in the Church of the members of Christ: the married, the widowed, the virginal. Because these kinds of life, these forms of chastity, were going to be found among the holy members of Christ, all three of them bore witness to Christ.

Let each of you choose from these three kinds of life whichever you wish.—*Sermon 196, 2*

PRAYER. *Come, Lord, let us love You and let us run to You.* —*Confessions VIII, 4, 9*

JULY 27
Let Us Come to the Dinner

LET us be done with vain or bad excuses; let us come to the dinner at which we can inwardly take our fill. Let us not be prevented by arrogance or pride; let no unlawful curiosity either lift us high with excitement or cast us down in terror, and in either case, turn us away from God.

Let no sensual voluptuousness divert us from heartfelt willingness. Let us come, let us take our fill. —*Sermon 112, 8*

PRAYER. *Let the beggars come because the one issuing the invitation is You Who became poor for our sakes.* —*Sermon 112, 8*

JULY 28
Fan This Spark of Good Love in Yourselves

IF my sermon has found in your hearts just a spark of the spontaneous love of God, nurse it carefully. Tell yourselves urgently to increase it by prayer, humility, the pain of repentance, the love of justice, good works, sincere sighs, a praiseworthy way of life, loyal friendship.

Fan this spark of good love in yourselves; nourish it in yourselves. —*Sermon 178, 11*

PRAYER. *O Love, ever burning, never extinguished! O Charity, my God.*

—*Confessions X, 29, 40*

JULY 29
The Two Kinds of Innocent Life

T O the best of your ability take a look at what this life holds—I'm not talking about a bad life, nor a wicked one, nor a criminal, nor a self-indulgent, nor an impious one; rather, I'm talking about the kind of innocent life one may expect Martha to have led. So take a look at that sort of life, as best you can, and think about it.

There remained in that house, which welcomed the Lord, two kinds of life in two women; both innocent, both praiseworthy; one laborious, the other leisurely.   —*Sermon 104, 4*

PRAYER.   *Lord, may we touch You in faith.*

—*Sermon 229I, 2*

JULY 30
The Scaffolding of Faith

S OMETHING was built in Christian faith, and certain temporary mechanical devices have been finished with. The fact that Christ rose again is over and done with; He isn't still rising again. And His ascending into heaven is over and done with.

The fact that in Him is also living forever that very nature of Humanity which He took, and in which He was willing to be born, willing to die in and be buried—all this is what has been built, all this remains forever.   —*Sermon 362, 7*

PRAYER.   *O God, You sent Your Son that by His example we might learn even a humility like His.*   —*Confessions X, 43, 68*

JULY 31
The Resurrection of the Dead

THE resurrection of the dead is our hope; the resurrection of the dead is our faith. It is also our charity, which blazes up at the proclamation of things that cannot yet be seen, and grows hot with a desire so huge that it gives our hearts the capacity to receive the bliss which is promised us for the future, enlarging them as long as they believe what they cannot yet see.

And so, take away faith in the resurrection of the dead, and the whole of Christian doctrine collapses. —*Sermon 361, 2*

PRAYER. *Let our minds, O God, be full of faith in the resurrection.* —*Sermon 242A, 3*

AUGUST 1
Two Days of a Good Life

AS someone who is wise, you are afraid you may no longer have two days of a good life. If tomorrow is one of them, let today be the other; let that be your two days.

If there isn't a tomorrow, then at least today will find you safe; and if there is a tomorrow for you, then it is added to today! —*Sermon 20, 4*

PRAYER. *Seeing that there is no way to flee from the Almighty, we turn round and flee to You, the Almighty.* —*On Ps. 88, 24*

AUGUST 2
How Do We Know God?

OW do we know God? From the things God has made. They all answer you, "Here we are; look, we're beautiful." Their beauty is their confession.

Who made these beautiful changeable things, if not One Who is beautiful and unchangeable? —*Sermon 241, 2*

PRAYER. *All these things of Your making are lovely, and lo, You Who made them are more lovely still, unutterably more.*

—*Confessions XIII, 20, 28*

AUGUST 3
Trusting God

OD does something. Why He does it —you either know and praise Him for it, or you don't know and trust Him, if you are upright of heart.

Being upright means praising God for things when you know the reasons, and not attributing foolishness to God when you don't know them. —*Sermon 15A, 8*

PRAYER. *If God is for us, who can be against us? Praise and glory to Him forever!*

—*Sermon 57*

AUGUST 4
Love, and the Lord Will Draw Near

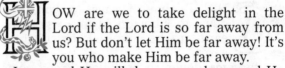

OW are we to take delight in the Lord if the Lord is so far away from us? But don't let Him be far away! It's you who make Him be far away.

Love, and He will draw near; love, and He will live with you. The Lord is very near; do not be anxious at all. —*Sermon 21, 2*

PRAYER. *O God, most high, most deep, most hidden yet intimately present, You are everywhere, whole and entire in every place, but confined to none.* —*Confessions VI, 3, 4*

AUGUST 5
To Love Peace Is To Have It

HAT a good thing it is to love peace! This, you see, is the same as having it. Is there anyone who doesn't wish what they love to increase?

If it's only a few people that you want to be at peace with you, then your peace will be small. If you want this possession to increase, add another possessor. —*Sermon 357, 2*

PRAYER. *I tasted You, and now I hunger and thirst for You. You touched me, and I burned for Your peace.* —*Confessions X, 27, 38*

AUGUST 6
Go Down To Labor on Earth

CHRIST Himself says to you, "Go down to labor on earth, to serve on earth, to be despised, crucified on earth."

Life came down, to be killed; Bread came down, to go hungry; the Way came down, to grow weary on a journey; the Fountain came down, to experience thirst; and are you refusing to endure toil? —*Sermon 78, 6*

PRAYER. *I labor here on this earth as though You had forgotten me even though I know well that You are only testing me and, even though You seem to cast me off, yet You will never fail to give me what You have promised.* —*On Ps. 87*

AUGUST 7
Love Life

E love life, and we have no hesitation at all about loving life; nor can we in the least deny that we love life. So let us choose life, if we love life.

What are we choosing? Life. First of all, here, a good one; after this one, the eternal kind.

—*Sermon 297, 8*

PRAYER. *You, God of my Love, for Whom I long that I may find strength: You are the Life of souls, the Life of all lives, the Life Who are Yourself living and unchanging, the Life of my own soul.* —*Confessions III, 6, 10*

AUGUST 8
Christ Is Your Mountain of Refuge

APPROACH the mountain, climb up the mountain, and you that climb it, don't go down it. There you will be safe, there you will be protected.

Christ is your mountain of refuge. And where is Christ? At the right hand of the Father, since He has ascended into heaven. —*Sermon 62A, 3*

PRAYER. *Because our souls were deeply disquieted within us we remembered You, O Lord, from our muddy Jordan; we called You to mind in that mountain which, although lofty as Yourself, was brought low for us. Disgusted with our darkness, we were converted to You.* —*Confessions XIII, 12, 13*

AUGUST 9
We Trust Him Who Is Our End

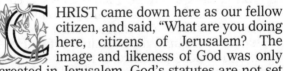CHRIST came down here as our fellow citizen, and said, "What are you doing here, citizens of Jerusalem? The image and likeness of God was only created in Jerusalem. God's statutes are not set up in this life. To work, in order to return.

"You ask 'How are we to return?' Here you are, I lay Myself under your feet, I become a Road for you, I will be the End for you. Imitate Me." —*Sermon 16A, 9*

PRAYER. *Make known to me, Lord, my end. I trust You Who are my End.* —*Sermon 16A, 9*

AUGUST 10
The Needy Are There in Front of Us

THE needy are there in front of us; if we deposit our savings with them, we won't lose them. We aren't afraid of anybody making off with them.

The One Who gave them to us, you see, is keeping them safe; nor could we find a better guardian, nor a more trustworthy maker and keeper of promises. —*Sermon 302, 8*

PRAYER. *Thanks be to You, our God! We belong to You as Your exhortations and consolations prove. And You are faithful to Your promises.* —*Confessions IX, 3, 5*

AUGUST 11
Thanks Be to God

THANKS be to Him to Whom we have been singing with devoted hearts and mouths "God, who is like You?" because we can feel the holy love of Him deeply ensconced in your hearts, because you revere Him as Lord, love Him as Father.

Thanks be to Him Who is desired before He is seen, and Whose presence is felt, and Whose coming is hoped for. Thanks be to Him, fear of Whom is not shaken off by love, love of Whom is not paralyzed by fear. He it is we bless and honor, both for you and in you. —*Sermon 24, 1*

PRAYER. *Let me recall with thanks, O God, Your mercies. May I be flooded with love for You until my bones cry out, "Who is like You, O Lord?"* —*Confessions VIII, 1, 1*

AUGUST 12
What You Shuddered at You Now Admire

OMEONE may say to me: "Those leaves have rotted, and new ones have been born." But even the leaves which rot yield themselves to the forces of the earth. What seemed to have been already used up and thrown away goes back into the richness of the earth, the richness into sap, the sap into the root.

What you shuddered at in the putrefaction of compost you admire in the fruit and greenery of the tree. —*Sermon 361, 11*

PRAYER. *O my Lord, water this barren soil of my dry and desolate soul with the infusion of Your grace.* —*"Like as the Hart"*

AUGUST 13
Seeking a Happy Life

HE Lord has magnified His Holy One to the extent of raising Him from the dead and giving Him the honor of sitting at His right hand in heaven. He has shown you what you should savor if you really wish to be happy.

In this life you cannot be happy. Nobody can. You're seeking a good thing, but the earth just isn't the region for the good thing you're seeking. What are you seeking? A completely happy life. Well, it isn't to be found here. —*Sermon 321, 5*

PRAYER. *I serve and worship You, my God, that I may be happy in You Who made me a being capable of happiness.* —*Confessions XIII, 1, 1*

AUGUST 14
We Shall See the Truth

"**B**LESSED are those who dwell in Your house; they will praise You forever and ever." There, our whole business will be praise of God. What will we praise if we haven't loved it? And what we have loved is what we shall see.

We shall see the truth, and God, Whom we shall be praising, will be that Truth. There we shall find what today we have sung: *Amen*, it is true; *alleluia*, praise the Lord. —*Sermon 236, 3*

PRAYER. *O gentle Truth, I strain to catch Your inner melody and hear You, that my joy may be perfect at the sound of the Bridegroom's voice.* —*Confessions IV, 15, 27*

AUGUST 15
Mothers of Christ

YOU became children; become mothers too. You were the mother's children when you were baptized; then you were born as members of Christ.

Bring whomever you can along to the bath of Baptism so that, just as you became children when you were born, you may likewise be able, by bringing others along to be born, to become mothers of Christ as well. —*Sermon 72A, 8*

PRAYER. *By the efforts of Your Saints, O God, Your Sacraments have made their way amid the waves of this world's temptations to the end that the peoples might be stamped with Your Name in Baptism.* —*Confessions XIII, 20, 26*

AUGUST 16
The True Image

HAT one looks for in an image is for it to be true, not vain. "Although man walks in the image," you see "that he is troubled in vain."

You see, it's by loving Truth that the image of God to which we were created is sculpted anew and his own proper coin is paid back to our Caesar. —*Sermon 90, 10*

PRAYER. *O Truth, illumination of my heart, let not my own darkness speak to me. Speak to me Yourself.* —*Confessions XII, 10, 10*

AUGUST 17
Fellow Disciples

HE office of master is dangerous; the state of disciple is safe. That's why the psalm says: "To my hearing You will give joy and exultation." Hearing the word is safer than uttering it.

So it is much safer that both we who speak and you who listen should realize that we are fellow disciples under one Master. Yes, it's unquestionably safer, and it helps you enormously, if you listen to us, not as your masters but as your fellow pupils. —*Sermon 23, 1-2*

PRAYER. *So speak that I may hear, Lord. My heart is listening. Open the ears of my heart and say to my soul: "I am Your salvation."*

—*Confessions I, 5, 5*

AUGUST 18
Who Is Your God?

HO is your God? The One Who made you. Who is the god of the smith? The one who made him. Who is the idol's god? The one who made it. So if the idol had a mind and heart, wouldn't it worship the smith?

There you are: that's the iniquity in which they have held down the truth and have not found the way leading to that possession which they have been able to see. —*Sermon 141, 3*

PRAYER. *How shall I come to You with an open face if I have worshiped another and offended You? If I were to die tomorrow, with what sort of face would I look upon You?* —*On Ps. 34, 14*

AUGUST 19
Keep Walking

E are Christians, and we all want to go on with the journey; and even if we don't want to, the journey is what in fact we have to go on with.

Nobody is permitted to stay here; all who come into this life are compelled by the turning wheel of time to pass on. There must be no room for idleness; keep walking, or you will be just dragged along. —*Sermon 346A, 1*

PRAYER. *When I fell, O God, You gave me Your hand. When I walked in Your ways, You walked with me; when I drew near to You, You welcomed me sweetly and tenderly.*—*Soliloquies XIII, 5*

AUGUST 20
Longing for Truth

HAT was Mary enjoying? What was she eating, what was she drinking so avidly with the mouth of her heart? Justice, truth. She was enjoying truth, listening to truth, avid for truth, longing for truth.

In her hunger she was eating truth, drinking it in her thirst. She was being refreshed, and what she was being fed from was not diminishing. —*Sermon 179, 5*

PRAYER. *In Your sweetness teach me so that truth may become sweet to me.* —*Sermon 153*

AUGUST 21
Living Rightly

IF you don't know what it is to live rightly, get to know the Divine commandments. Perhaps, after all, there are many people who do live rightly, but the reason nobody seems to you to live rightly is that you are ignorant of what living rightly means.

If however you do know, act on what you know, so that you yourself may have what you are looking for and may also show others something to imitate. —*Sermon 351, 11*

PRAYER. *Let me not be my own life! In You I begin to live again.* —*Confessions XII, 10, 10*

AUGUST 22
Give, and You Will Be Given

GOD treats his beggar in the way that you treat yours; so "give, and you will be given." If you are not willing to do so, look out for yourself.

The poor man is crying out and saying to you: "I'm asking for bread and you don't give it to me; you're asking for life and not getting it." —*Sermon 350C, 1*

PRAYER. *O Lord, you will heap gift after gift upon me, that my soul will shake itself free from the sticky morass of concupiscence and follow me to You.* —*Confessions X, 30, 42*

AUGUST 23
The Word Is Whole for All

WHAT must be the case with the Word that makes everything? It's like this voice of mine, all of it for each of all my listeners, the whole of it remaining with each of you.

And yet I haven't got as many voices as you have ears, but one voice fills many ears, not shared out among them but all of it in all of them. Well, think of God's Word in the same way. —*Sermon 28, 4*

PRAYER. *Let me listen to You Who are Truth; bring the ear of my heart close to the word of Your mouth.* —*Confessions IV, 5, 10*

AUGUST 24
Our Nets Mean Life

THE "nets" we are called to spread for others mean life; only let love be maintained. And don't consider how irksome you are to a person but how lovable that person is to you.

What sort of loving care are you showing if you spare someone and they die?—*Sermon 400, 11*

PRAYER. *O my God, Loftiness in my lowliness and Rest in my labor, You Who hear my confessions and forgive my sins, You command me to love my neighbor as myself.*—*Confessions XII, 26, 36*

AUGUST 25
Those Who Ask Are the Same as Those They Are Asking

WE should consider, when we are asked for something, who they are that are doing the asking, and from whom they are asking for it. Who are doing the asking? Human beings. From whom are they asking for it? From human beings. Who are doing the asking? Fragile creatures. Who are doing the asking? Poor wretches. From whom are they asking for it? From poor wretches! —*Sermon 61, 8*

PRAYER. *Let the haughty laugh at me, those who have never yet been flat on their faces, felled for their own good by You, my God; but let me confess my disgraceful deeds to You, and in confessing praise You. Without You, what am I but a guide to my own downfall?*

—*Confessions IV, 1, 1*

AUGUST 26

We Brought Nothing into the World, but Neither Can We Take Anything Out

OTHING did we bring into this world. But perhaps because you brought nothing and found much when you were here, you are going to take something away with you from here?

So listen to this as well. Let the Apostle say this also, since he has no mind to flatter you: "We brought nothing into this world," when we were born, of course; "but neither can we take anything out," of course, when we leave the world.

—Sermon 61, 9

PRAYER. *My God, I would not exist, I would not be at all, were You not in me, or rather were I not in You.* *—Confessions I, 2, 2*

AUGUST 27

She Knew How To Keep because She Was Not Afraid To Lose

THE mother of the Maccabees knew how to keep and preserve her sons. She knew how to keep because she was not afraid of losing them.

Each of them suffered by feeling pain in himself; she, by seeing what was done, suffered in all of them. She watched them dying and loved them all; she endured in her eyes what they all endured in the flesh. *—Sermon 300, 6*

PRAYER. *No one loses You unless he tries to get rid of You. He alone loses no one dear to him to whom all are dear in God Who is never lost.*

—Confessions IV, 9, 14

AUGUST 28

The Wealth We Share in Common Is Our Lord

 E all belong to one great household and are all under one Head of the Family. He has an ample storeroom from which both we and you are able to live.

What I live on is what I utter to you; what I'm fed on is what I serve up to you. Because with you I am poor. The wealth we share in common is our Lord: the life of us all, blessed and eternal. —*Sermon 319A*

PRAYER. *O incarnate wisdom, God of Truth, You call to all humankind and cry out to them: I am your food and the goal of your happiness.*
—*Soliloquies XIII, 4*

AUGUST 29

Preserving Unity for the Body of Christ

"NEW commandment I give to you, that you should love one another." While our Lord is making Himself a Body out of us all, as from His members, a Body with one Head, you are busy wrenching yourselves away from the members of Christ and have no love for unity.

So why not seek to be put right yourself, to be fetched back into the community of Christ's members, and to fit harmoniously into His Body, yes, you too? —*Sermon 400, 8*

PRAYER. *O my Divine Head in Whom all the light of wisdom abides, guide me; O light of my inward eye, enlighten me; O divine unity, make me meek and gentle.* —*Soliloquies I, 8*

AUGUST 30
Be Still and See

NE thing "have I begged from the Lord, this will I seek"; not the many things I'm busy with, but "that I may dwell in the house of the Lord through all the days of my life, that I may gaze upon the delight of the Lord."

That is not the bliss of people who work themselves to the bone! "Be still and see"— what?—"that I am the Lord": a tremendous vision, inexhaustibly satisfying contemplation.

—*Sermon 104, 7*

PRAYER. *Let me seek You, Lord, even while I am calling upon You, and call upon You even as I believe in You.* —*Confessions I, 1, 1*

AUGUST 31
Do Not Be Ashamed of Revealing Where You Feel Pain

HE Pharisee was not rejoicing so much in his own clean bill of health as in comparing it with the diseases of others. It would have been more worth his while, since he had come to the Doctor, to inform Him by confession of the things that were wrong with him.

So it's not surprising that it was the tax-collector who went away cured since he had not been ashamed of showing where he felt pain. —*Sermon 351, 1*

PRAYER. *Is Your hand not powerful enough to heal all my soul's ills, O all-powerful God?*

—*Confessions X, 30, 42*

SEPTEMBER 1
You Reach God by Humility

IN ordinary, visible situations, in order to reach places high up, you stretch yourself up to your full height. God, however, though He is the most sublimely high up of all things, is not reached by hoisting oneself up but by humbling oneself.

This is why the prophet says: "The Lord is near to those who have crushed their hearts."

—Sermon 351, 1

PRAYER. *In Your unfathomable mercy You first gave the humble certain pointers to the true Mediator, and then sent Him, that by His example they might learn even a humility like His.* *—Confessions X, 43, 68*

SEPTEMBER 2
Let Your Last Day Find You Still Fighting

ONLY aim at going forward, not backward. If your last day does not find you victorious, let it find you at least still fighting, not captured and tied up. *—Sermon 22, 8*

PRAYER. *From oppression and violence the Lord redeems all who believe in Him, all who say to Him from the heart: "I believe I shall see the Lord's goodness in the land of the living."* *—Sermon 216*

131

SEPTEMBER 3
Love Your Neighbor as Yourself

I F I have to love God with the whole of what is alive in me, what will I leave myself to love my neighbor with? You see, when you were instructed about loving your neighbor, you weren't told "with the whole heart, soul, and mind" but "as yourself."

You must love God with the whole of you, because He is better than you are; your neighbor as yourself, because he is the same as you are.

—*Sermon 179A, 3*

PRAYER. *It is out of love for loving You that I pray.*
—*Confessions XI, 1, 1*

SEPTEMBER 4
God Is Our Helper in the Fight

O NE pleasurable habit may be dead, but another is very much alive; and this one, too, as long as you don't consent to it, you are putting to death. When it begins not to be pleasurable at all, you have put it to death.

While we are wrestling in this contest, we have God as a spectator; when we are in trouble, we can ask for God as our helper. Because if He doesn't help us Himself, we won't be able, I don't say to win, but even to fight.
—*Sermon 156, 9*

PRAYER. *Let God arise; let Him take up His arms; let Him rise up to help us. He makes of our soul whatever suits His purpose. When it is in His hand, let Him use it as He wills.*

—*On Ps. 33, 4, 3*

SEPTEMBER 5
Walk by the Spirit

HEN you begin to find the going hard in your fight against the lusts of the flesh, walk by the Spirit, call upon the Spirit, start seeking the gift of God.

And if the law of your members is fighting back against the law of your mind from the lower part—that is, from the flesh—and is holding you captive under the law of sin, even that will be corrected. All you have to do is call upon Him. *—Sermon 163, 12*

PRAYER. *Let us call on the Spirit constantly, calling on Him for help, that we may hear Him saying to our souls: "I am your salvation."*

—Sermon 163, 12

SEPTEMBER 6
To the Heart the Door Is Opened

T'S no use our hammering on the Lord's door with stones or crowbars, with fists or feet. Life knocks, and to Life the door is opened.

It is with the heart one asks, with the heart one seeks, with the heart one knocks, and to the heart the door is opened. *—Sermon 91, 3*

PRAYER. *I am knocking in the earnestness of my heart at the door of my Lord God that He may deign to unravel the mystery.—On Ps. 31, 1*

SEPTEMBER 7
Christal the Road

"SET a guard over my mouth while the sinner stood up against me." Christ became the Way, the Road, for you. But "whoever say that they abide in Christ ought themselves to walk even as He walked."

He is the Roadway. So let us walk now, unafraid. Do not let us go astray; do not let us walk off the Road. —*Sermon 16A, 10*

PRAYER. *O Truth, is there any road where You have not walked with me, teaching me what to avoid and what to aim at?* —*Confessions X, 40, 65*

SEPTEMBER 8
What Cannot Be Spoken Can Yet Be Believed

ONDERFUL to relate, what we are not capable of expressing we are not permitted to pass over in silence. We proclaim out loud in words what we cannot comprehend in the silence of our thoughts. Indeed, we are unable to express this stupendous gift of God because we are too little to explain His greatness, and yet we are obliged to praise Him lest, by keeping silent, we should remain ungrateful.

But thank God that what cannot be suitably spoken can be faithfully believed. —*Sermon 215, 3*

PRAYER. *Your judgments, O Lord, are a great depth; Your judgments are incomprehensible. May we learn wisdom, may we learn faith, while depth calls upon depth.* —*"Like as the Hart"*

SEPTEMBER 9
The Inner Teacher

GET the inner inhabitant behind your inner eyes on his feet; let him take to his windows and inspect God's creation.

Thus, it is not the eyes that see, but there is someone who sees through the eyes. Get him on his feet; wake him up; you haven't been denied such a lodger, after all. —*Sermon 126, 3*

PRAYER. *O Divine Word Who created all that is in heaven and on earth, and uphold Your creation by Your strength and providence: You begin, Lord, to have pity on me; You make a ray of Your mercy, beauty, wisdom shine out in my soul.* —*Soliloquies VI, 3*

SEPTEMBER 10
God's Healing Chastisement

DON'T let God's chastisements get you down or He may leave you alone so that you perish forever. Let us stick it out, this saving medicine of His, and not run away from His scourge.

That is what He is teaching us with; that is what He is warning us with; that is how He is building us up. —*Sermon 113A, 14*

PRAYER. *See how my soul is showing You its sores, begging You to heal them. It longs for perfect health so as to confess all the benefits I have received from You from the first moment of my life until this moment when I dare to pray to You.* —*Soliloquies XIII, 4*

SEPTEMBER 11
In the Sight of God We Ought To Be Doers

YOU are hearers of the word; we are its preachers. Inwardly, though, we are all hearers. Inwardly, in the heart, in the mind, where He is teaching you Who prompts you to applaud.

I am speaking outwardly; He is arousing you inwardly. So we are all hearers inwardly and all of us, both outwardly and inwardly, in the sight of God ought to be doers. —*Sermon 179, 7*

PRAYER. *I do not seek anything outside the Lord but the Lord Himself, and He will hear me and, even as I am speaking, He will say: "Here am I."*
—*On Ps. 33, 2, 9*

SEPTEMBER 12
Christ Is the Way

TO keep to the middle way, the true, straight road, between despair and presumption, would be extremely difficult for us unless Christ Himself had said: "I am the Way."

"I am," He says, "the Way, the Truth, and the Life." As though to say: How do you want to go? "I am the Way." Where do you want to go? "I am the Truth." Where do you want to stay? "I am the Life." —*Sermon 142, 1*

PRAYER. *You, O Christ, are the Light without darkness, the Sun without spot, the Way without turning, the Truth without error, the Life without flaw, Happiness without end or limit.*
—*Soliloquies IV, 2*

SEPTEMBER 13
How To Possess Your Wealth

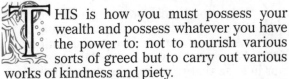

HIS is how you must possess your wealth and possess whatever you have the power to: not to nourish various sorts of greed but to carry out various works of kindness and piety.

Thus, you will wait for the last day without anxiety, genuinely rich, inwardly rich, outwardly as best you can, inwardly as you have been commanded. —*Sermon 299E, 5*

PRAYER. *Let us return thanks for the power which is given us, and pray that our weakness may not lead us astray.* —*John's Gospel 53, 5*

SEPTEMBER 14
Delight in the One Who Hangs There

OU are a Christian; you carry on your forehead the Cross of Christ; the mark stamped on you teaches you what you should profess.

When He was hanging on the Cross—the Cross you carry on your forehead—He was looking round at the people raving against Him: putting up with their insults, praying for His enemies. So don't delight in the sign of the wood but in the sign of the One hanging on it. —*Sermon 302, 3*

PRAYER. *Do you call upon Jesus and think that you are not whole?* —*Sermon 174, 3*

SEPTEMBER 15
Jesus Gave Us an Example of Patience

I N the things that our Lord suffered from His enemies, He was pleased to give us an example of patience for our salvation and also for our advantage in the way we lead our lives so that we ourselves should not refuse to suffer the same sort of things, if that should be His will, for the honor of the Gospel.

The fact is that not even in His mortal flesh did He suffer anything out of necessity but everything of His own free will. —*Sermon 218, 1.10*

PRAYER. *Let us beseech Him to say to our souls, "I am your salvation." No other salvation will I seek but the Lord my God.* —*On Ps. 34, 6*

SEPTEMBER 16
St. Cyprian, Sign of Unity

T O Him be praise, to Him be glory, Who was pleased to create Cyprian at an opportune time, teach him in his obedience, guide him in his teaching, aid him in his fight, and crown him in his victory.

To Him be praise, to Him be glory, Who made this man a figure in whom to demonstrate to His Church to what great evils charity was to be opposed and to what great goods it was to be preferred, and how there could be no charity in a Christian who did not cherish and protect the unity of Christ. —*Sermon 312, 6*

PRAYER. *O Body of Christ, holy Church, let all that is within you say, "Lord, who is like You?"*
—*On Ps. 34, 14*

SEPTEMBER 17
God Never Loses His Charm

HOLD on to God because He never loses His charm, because there is nothing more lovely than He. The reason that other things lose their charm is that they cannot last, that they are not as He is.

Nothing, O human soul, nothing after all can be enough for you but the One Who created you. —*Sermon 125, 11*

PRAYER. *O God, my hope from my youth, was it not You Who created me?* —*Confessions VI, 1, 1*

SEPTEMBER 18
The Gifts of God

GOD gave us our nature so that we might exist; gave us the soul so that we might live; gave us the mind so that we might understand; gave us foodstuffs to sustain this mortal life; gave us light from the sky, springs from the earth. But all these things are gifts common to good and bad alike. Does that mean that He hasn't kept anything special for the good?

He certainly does keep something! And what is that something that He keeps for the good? "What eye has not seen, nor ear heard, nor the human heart conceived." —*Sermon 331, 3*

PRAYER. *Let us lift up our hearts to that which eye has not seen, nor ear heard, nor the human heart conceived.* —*Cf. Sermon 331, 3*

SEPTEMBER 19
True Life

TRUTH, the real Truth, is promising us a life which is not only eternal but also blessed, where there's no nuisance to annoy, no toil, no fear, no grief.

What you find there is full and total and definitive freedom from anxiety. Life under God, life with God, life coming from God, life which is God Himself. —*Sermon 297, 8*

PRAYER. What have You commanded, O Lord my God? I have sought advice on life. What life, if not that of which it is said: "In You is the fountain of life." —*On St John's Gospel, Tr. 34*

SEPTEMBER 20
If You Had Gold, How Would You Use It?

YOU are saying: "I am sorry for the gold that comes in that person's way. Oh, if only I had it!" What would you do with it? "I would take in strangers, feed the needy, clothe the naked, redeem captives." Fine talk before you have it, but how will you talk when you do have it?

If you really use gold like that, because you love Him more by Whom the gold was created, then you will be upright, loving higher things more, using lower things rightly. —*Sermon 21, 10*

PRAYER. Let Your creation praise You so that we may love You, and let us love You so that praise may be offered to You by Your creation.
—*Confessions XIII, 33, 48*

SEPTEMBER 21
God Serves Us

E serve God, and God serves us. When I said: "We serve God," everyone agreed. But when I said, "God serves us," I may have shocked some people.

We serve Him, not He us, surely? Yet it is good for us that He should serve us by cultivating us because, unless He cultivates or serves this field, it will get full of thistles. —*Sermon 125A, 5*

PRAYER. *May I serve You on earth as the angels serve You in heaven, lovingly carrying out all Your commands and never offending You.*

—*Sermon 56*

SEPTEMBER 22
The Poor Have Been Appointed Our Comrades

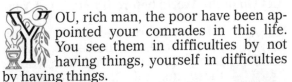OU, rich man, the poor have been appointed your comrades in this life. You see them in difficulties by not having things, yourself in difficulties by having things.

In not having things, they have nothing to support them; you, in having much, have what weighs you down. Supply their lack and diminish your load. —*Sermon 25A, 4*

PRAYER. *My God, stir up and animate in me the desire to pay back what I so truly owe You. Teach me how great that love must be which You command me to have for You.*

—*Soliloquies VII, 1*

SEPTEMBER 23
He Wants To Give

I T'S on the Lord's own door that you must knock, where His household is at rest with Him. You must knock by praying, asking, insisting. He's not like that friend in the parable who will only get up and give it to you when he can't stand that racket any longer. He really wants to give.

While you are knocking you have not yet received. Go on knocking; He wants to give.

—*Sermon 105, 3*

PRAYER. *Let us ask of You, seek in You, knock at Your door. Only so will we receive, only so find, only so will the door be opened to us.* —*Confessions XIII, 38, 53*

SEPTEMBER 24
Let Go of the World before It Lets Go of You

A IM your hearts and minds at God. Don't deceive yourselves. When things are going well with you in the world, that's the time to interrogate yourselves, that's the time to ask whether you love this world or not.

Learn how to let go of it before it lets go of you. What do I mean by 'letting go'? Not loving it with all your heart. —*Sermon 125, 11*

PRAYER. *Let us implore God that the heart may be inwardly aroused and cleansed, for it is within the heart that petition is made to God Himself.* —*Sermon 11, 11*

SEPTEMBER 25
Loving God Freely

THE Psalmist said, "O Lord, why give me an inheritance? Whatever You give, it isn't worth much. You be my inheritance; I love You; I love You with all my mind; I love You. What can it mean to me, anything You give me apart from Yourself?"

This is what it means to love God freely, to hope in God for God, to hasten to be filled with God, to be satisfied with Him. —*Sermon 334, 3*

PRAYER. *What can be given to me that is better than God? God loves me; God loves each one. See, He has made the offer, "Ask what you will."* —*On Ps. 33, 3*

SEPTEMBER 26
The Sickness of the World

HOW would we cope if such a great Comforter were not present? The human race was gravely ill, from Adam right up to the end.

From the moment we are born here, life is clearly an illness. But at the end this was going to become more serious, with a possibility of taking a turn toward a recovery of health, and for some toward death. So since the human race was so ill, that great Doctor takes over the care of the patient. —*Sermon 346A, 8*

PRAYER. *Lord, have mercy on me! You are the Physician, and I am sick; You are merciful, and I am in need of mercy.* —*Confessions X, 28, 39*

SEPTEMBER 27
God Surpasses All

UNDERSTAND and savor wisely what you have heard. Consider how great and wonderful it is and take care to think even more grandly about God.

He surpasses all light and all sound, He surpasses all meaning and understanding.

—*Sermon 28, 5*

PRAYER. *You are most high, excellent, omnipotent, supremely merciful and supremely just, most hidden yet intimately present, infinitely beautiful and infinitely strong, steadfast yet elusive, unchanging Yourself though You control the change in all things.* —*Confessions I, 4, 4*

SEPTEMBER 28
It's the Cause, Not the Punishment, That Makes the Martyr

CHOOSE the cause, and you won't have to worry about the punishment. But if you don't choose the right cause, you will find punishment both here and in the next world.

Don't let yourself be confused by the penalties undergone by malefactors, by the sacrilegious, by the foes of peace and the enemies of truth. They aren't dying for the truth, but to stop the truth being proclaimed. —*Sermon 325, 2*

PRAYER. *What am I to confess, Lord, in this field of temptation? What indeed, except that I take more delight in truth than in any eulogy.*

—*Confessions X, 37, 61*

SEPTEMBER 29
Through Increasing Our Capacity
We Will Be Filled in Due Course

I T'S the business of human beings living this mortal life to hunger and thirst for justice. But to be filled with justice belongs to that other life.

The angels have their fill of this bread, this food; human beings, however, in being hungry for it stretch themselves; in stretching themselves they are enlarged; in being enlarged they increase their capacity; through increasing their capacity they will be filled in due course.
— *Sermon 400, 1*

PRAYER. *We ask for that which we may possess forever, that through which we shall never again be in want. Let us hunger and thirst so that we may be filled with that for which we are asking.* — *Sermon 61*

SEPTEMBER 30
Hold On to Charity

I F there's no time or leisure to pore over all the sacred pages, to leaf through all the volumes of the words they contain, to penetrate all the secrets of the Scriptures, hold on to charity, on which they all depend.
— *Sermon 350, 2*

PRAYER. *O my God, how amazingly deep are Your Scriptures! To look into that depth makes me shudder, but it is the shudder of awe, the trembling of love.* — *Confessions XII, 14, 17*

OCTOBER 1
Let Us Live like Exiles

THE Lord is ever so high above; take good care of your wings. Believe what you can't yet see so that you may earn the right to see what you believe.

Let us live like exiles; let us think of ourselves as transients passing through, and we will sin the less. —*Sermon 301, 9*

PRAYER. *Make me possess You, O eternal Happiness of our minds and bodies: to see and feel You in the center of my heart, O blessed Life and ineffable Sweetness of my soul.* —*Soliloquies I, 1*

OCTOBER 2
True Faith Is Spiritual

TRUE faith is spiritual; it is believing that your Lord is your protector in the present time so that you may come to what is beyond time.

It is hoping that you will live the life of angels, not in carnal corruptions, not in pleasures and excitements, not in fornication and drunkenness and the enjoyment of carnal revels, not in the pride of earthly power—but just the kind of life that angels live. —*Sermon 4, 3*

PRAYER. *Grant to us Your Christ; let us know Your Christ and see Your Christ, just as the angels look upon Him and are glad.* —*On Ps. 84*

OCTOBER 3
The Good Life

 HAT is a good life? To love God with all your heart and soul and mind and to love your brother or sister as yourself.

So let us love our God and let us love each other in His unity, so that when Christ our Lord comes Himself we can say: "Lord, with Your help we have done what You commanded; by Your gracious favor may we receive what You have promised."—*Sermon 154A, 6*

PRAYER. *What does one who loves God say? O magnify the Lord with me! I will not be alone in magnifying the Lord, I will not be alone in loving Him, I will not be alone in embracing Him.* —*On Ps. 33, 6*

OCTOBER 4
Be Still in Your Heart

 RE you a lover of peace? Be still there in your heart with your Beloved. "And what am I to do?" There's plenty you can do. Put a stop to wrangling, and turn to prayer.

Don't repel with abuse those who are abusing you but pray for them. You want to speak against them? Instead, speak to God for them. —*Sermon 357, 4*

PRAYER. *Have we not mutual need of one another's prayers? For reciprocal prayers are enkindled by charity and are fragrant and pleasing to You, O Lord.* —*Sermon 13*

OCTOBER 5
Don't Find Fault

YOU, a person in charge of your own household, are unfairly and foolishly blamed by someone who is ignorant of your reasons and your plans. And have you the nerve to find fault with the One in charge of the whole universe, the Creator of heaven and earth, because the wind has blown up and withered the vines or a thundercloud has sprung up and poured down hail?

Don't find fault. He knows both how to control and how to arrange all His works.

—*Sermon 15A, 8*

PRAYER. *O Truth, Your best servants are less intent on hearing from You what they will and more on willing what they hear from You.*

—*Confessions X, 26, 37*

OCTOBER 6
Live Good Lives and You Will Change the Times

LIVE good lives and, by living good lives, you will change the times. You will change the times and then you'll have nothing to grumble about.

What, after all, are the times, my dear brothers and sisters? The spacing and unrolling of the ages.

—*Sermon 311, 8*

PRAYER. *You, O Lord, are sweet; teach me in Your sweetness! Only then shall I learn how to act if You teach me in Your sweetness.*

—*Sermon 153*

OCTOBER 7
The Source Is Not Closed if the Heart Is Open

 HY go looking for gold with such laborious travels? Love these riches instead, and you are filled with them right now. Their source is not closed if your heart is open.

The heart is opened by the key of faith: it both opens and cleans up the place you put it in. Don't think of yourself as too cramped and narrow. Your riches, your God, when He comes in, will widen and enlarge you. —*Sermon 177, 4*

PRAYER. *Open my heart, You Who are called the Key of David, Who reign sovereignly over our hearts and Who open them when it pleases You.* —*Soliloquies VII, 2*

OCTOBER 8
Rich and Poor Are in Need of Each Other

ERHAPS you can find someone poor who does not need the patrimony of the rich. But you certainly won't find anyone rich who isn't also in need of the patrimony of the poor. It was the patrimony of the poor that Job lost when he was smitten with terrible sores from head to foot.

Yet he wasn't induced to ascribe folly to God and, in his troubles, to be displeased with God. He was always pleased with God. —*Sermon 359A, 6*

PRAYER. *Hear my prayer, O Lord; do not let my soul faint under Your discipline nor let me fail in recounting to You Your mercies.*
—*Confessions I, 15, 24*

OCTOBER 9
Listen to the Words You Speak

PAY attention to the words coming out of your mouth. Listen, not to me but to yourself. Notice to Whom we say "Our Father, Who art in heaven."

It isn't just a friend, just a neighbor, but the very One to Whom we say this, that is commanding us to reach agreement. Together, in the presence of the Father, we have one voice; why don't we together have one peace?

—*Sermon 357, 4*

PRAYER. *Let us rid our hearts of all poison by calling on the Name of the Savior.*

—*On the Creed for the Catechumens*

OCTOBER 10
Those Who Throw Themselves Down before Him Will Be Raised Up

ANY who refuse to humble themselves in repentance should not think they can draw near to God. It is one thing, after all, to raise oneself up to God; it is another thing to raise oneself up against God.

Those who throw themselves down before Him are raised up by Him; those who raise themselves up against Him are thrown down by Him. —*Sermon 351, 1*

PRAYER. *I am in trouble here below while You dwell above, O God. Should I exalt myself, then You will remain aloof; but if I humble myself, then You will bend down Your ear to hear me.* —*On Ps. 101*

OCTOBER 11
Tribulation Makes for Patience

MAY God in His mercy grant that we may be shaken every day, or tempted or tested or tried, in order that we may make some progress.

"Tribulation makes for patience; patience for approval; approval for hope. As for hope, it doesn't let us down." —*Sermon 16A, 12*

PRAYER. *O God, in Your mercy, grant that I may be shaken every day!* —*Cf. Sermon 16A, 12*

OCTOBER 12
What Earns Sight Is Faith

BELIEVING is one thing, seeing is another. Believe because you don't see in order that, by believing what you cannot see, you may deserve to see what you believe.

What earns sight is faith; what rewards faith is sight. Why look for the reward before the work? So believe then, and walk in faith. Your salvation lies in hope. —*Sermon 97A, 2*

PRAYER. *How great is the abundance of the goodness which God hides for those who fear Him, which He perfects for those who hope in Him!* —*Sermon 194, 3*

OCTOBER 13
God Himself Is Our Reward

GOD Himself will be our reward, without Whom the rich are only beggars, and with Whom the poor are superabundantly rich.

What, after all, do the rich possess if they do not possess God? What do the poor not possess if they do possess God?—*Sermon 350C, 2*

PRAYER. *Needy and poor am I, O Lord, but I am the better for recognizing it and lamenting it in secret, and seeking Your mercy until my shortcomings are made good and my imperfect self brought to perfection in a peace which the gaze of the arrogant will never know.* —*Confessions. X, 38, 63*

OCTOBER 14
Put Your Heart Where You Say You Do

LET'S make absolutely sure that we don't hear the words "Lift up your hearts" to no purpose. Why place our hearts on earth when we can see how the earth is being turned upside down?

All I can do is to urge you to put your hearts where you say you do and to give an answer for your hope to those who taunt and blaspheme you for bearing the Name of Christ. —*Sermon 105, 11*

PRAYER. *Behold me here before You, O my God; see that I do not lie. As my speech is, so is my heart.* —*Confessions XI, 25, 32*

OCTOBER 15
Confess Your Sins

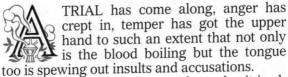

A TRIAL has come along, anger has crept in, temper has got the upper hand to such an extent that not only is the blood boiling but the tongue too is spewing out insults and accusations.

Don't you see to where, on the rocks, it is already hurling you? See! for God's sake, and put it right! Say: "I've done wrong"; say: "I've sinned." You won't die if you say this; you certainly will die if you don't say it.   *—Sermon 17, 6*

PRAYER. *Now I understand, O Source of all good, the extent of my malice when I have abandoned and forgotten You. —Soliloquies V, 5*

OCTOBER 16
Pursue Charity

P URSUE charity, the sweet and salutary bond of our minds, without which the rich are poor and with which the poor are rich.

Charity endures in adversity, is moderate in prosperity, brave under sufferings, cheerful in good works, reliable in temptation, open-handed in hospitality, as happy as can be among true brothers and sisters, as patient as you can get among false ones.   *—Sermon 350, 2*

PRAYER. *O Lord my God, may Your mercy grant my longing, a longing on fire not for myself alone but to serve the brothers and sisters I dearly love. —Confessions XI, 2, 3*

OCTOBER 17
When We Forgive, We Also Are Forgiven

LET us go on and on praying that God will forgive; but let us do what it says—let's also forgive our own debtors ourselves. When we forgive, we also are forgiven.

We can say this every day and it can happen to us every day. —*Sermon 181, 8*

PRAYER. *What thanks shall I render You, O Lord, for making clear to me in Your light the depths of wretchedness and nothingness into which I have been cast by sin?* —*Soliloquies V, 5*

OCTOBER 18
What Lives in Your Heart?

LET us question divine charity and let us set before her the two kinds of human charity. The person who chooses to stay with that lawful human love does not stay with the unlawful sort. If you have them both by admitting into yourself the love of a harlot, you are doing wrong to the divine charity who is living there.

Are you then going to bring the love of a harlot along to live in your heart together with the love of God, and offend the honor of the Blood of Christ? —*Sermon 349, 4*

PRAYER. *The Lord says to you: "Behold I am here. What do you desire? What do you ask of Me? Anything I can give is much less than Myself. Possess Me, enjoy Me, embrace Me.*

—*On Ps. 33, 9*

OCTOBER 19
Everything Can Be Endured for Love

ALL ought to say in their tribulations: "The Lord is my strength" and "I will love You, Lord, my might." Love is itself might, or courage.

I mean, if you really know how to love, you can endure anything and everything for what you love. —*Sermon 299E, 1*

PRAYER. *By Your mercy, O Lord, You plucked me from all my evil ways. I long for You to grow sweeter to me than all those allurements I was pursuing. You have enabled me to love You with all my strength and with passionate yearning grasp Your hand, so that You may rescue me from every temptation until my life's end.* —*Confessions I, 15, 24*

OCTOBER 20
We Owe All to Christ

IT is to Christ that we owe the fact that we are, that we live, that we have understanding, that we are human, that we have lived good lives, that we have understood things rightly: we owe it all to Him.

Of our own, there's nothing that we have except sin. —*Sermon 176, 6*

PRAYER. *May Your will be done in me and by me; let me never resist Your will, and let there be no barrier between us.* —*Sermon 56*

OCTOBER 21
Lose Your Soul for Love

DO you love your soul? Lose it. But you'll say to me, "How can I deliberately lose what I love?"

By the very fact of loving life, pour out your life. By the very fact of loving your soul, lose it. Because when you lose it for God's sake in the present time, you will find it in the time to come for eternal life. So, by the very fact of loving life, pour it out.

—Sermon 313D, 2

PRAYER. *Have pity on me and show me Your goodness; put Your power into effect to produce divine life in my soul.* *—Soliloquies VI, 2*

OCTOBER 22
Let Us Take Care of Christ

LET us take care of Christ. He's with us in those who are His; He's with us in ourselves. Nor was it to no purpose that He said: "Behold, I am with you always until the consummation of the world."

By doing this sort of thing we recognize Christ in good works, with the heart, not the body; not with eyes of the body but with the eyes of faith. *—Sermon 239, 7*

PRAYER. *Let us cry out to Christ Who is passing by, not with our words but with our works.* *—Sermon 349, 5*

OCTOBER 23
Christian Hope

AS long as we are in this world, if we take care to have our hearts lifted up above, the fact that we are walking here below won't be to our disadvantage.

We are walking here below, after all, in this flesh. So, by fixing our hope up above, we have set it like an anchor on firm ground.

—*Sermon 359A, 1*

PRAYER. *O Lord our God, grant us to trust in Your overshadowing wings: protect us beneath them and bear us up. While we are absent our home falls not to ruins, for our home is Your eternity.* —*Confessions IV, 16, 31*

OCTOBER 24
Look Up and See the Beauty of God

LOOK up and observe what a difference there is between your money and your God. The sun in the sky is more beautiful than your money, and yet this sun is not your God.

Accordingly, if this sunlight is more beautiful than your money, how much more beautiful must He be by Whom this sunlight was made? —*Sermon 399, 10*

PRAYER. *Where are You, O Beauty so hidden and invisible, that I may make known to You the wounds and desires of my love? For I shall never be wholly satisfied until I see You face to face.* —*Soliloquies I, 6*

OCTOBER 25
Christic the Sower

HRIST was sowing, and the Church sprung up. The grain fell; the grain rose again; and the grain ascended into heaven. Now there is a multitude of grains. —*Sermon 335E, 2*

PRAYER. The mercy You show to the Saints, O Lord, is heavenly, not earthly; it is eternal, not temporal. And how have You made it known to us? In that Your truth reaches even to the clouds. —*On Ps. 35, 8*

OCTOBER 26
Transport Your Longing to Where You Are To Follow

HERE is another life, my brothers and sisters; there is, believe me, another life after this life. Prepare yourselves for it; be indifferent to all the present life has to offer.

If you are provided with it, do good with it. If you aren't, don't burn yourselves up with greedy longings. Transport it, transfer it ahead of you. Let what you have here go on up there where you are going to follow.

—*Sermon 311, 15*

PRAYER. Behold I am here, says the Lord, what do you want? What do you ask of Me? Whatever I give you is of less worth than Myself. —*On Ps. 33, 1*

OCTOBER 27
Yearn for Life

EARN for life and love to see good days where there will be no night; life in which no evil day is to be feared; good days in which life will never end.

But if you love this reward then beware of refusing the work whose reward it is. Attend to that peace by seeking her. Seek her with your hands in the night before God, and you will not be disappointed. —*Sermon 16, 5*

PRAYER. *Lord, when I at last cling to You with my whole being, there will be no more grief or toil. My life will be alive, filled wholly with You.* —*Confessions X, 28, 39*

OCTOBER 28
"Without Me You Can Do Nothing"

ET our way be directed toward the Lord. It is a narrow way, a thorny way, a rough way; but, with the passage of so many and such wonderful feet, it has become smooth.

The Lord went along it first; the Apostles went along it fearlessly; after them the Martyrs, boys, women, girls. But who was within them? "Without Me you can do nothing." —*Sermon 295, 8*

PRAYER. *You are a refuge for raising up and directing Your children, O Lord. And still You are giving good gifts. For You deal with us gently lest we faint by the way and reprove us lest we wander from the right way.*
—*Sermon on the Mount 55, 6*

OCTOBER 29
Christ in Heaven, Christ on Earth

BSERVE the loving affection of this Head of ours. He is already in heaven, and He is struggling here on earth as long as the Church is struggling here.

Christ is hungry here, thirsty here; He's naked; He's a migrant; He's sick; He's in prison. You see, whatever His Body suffers here He suffers too. —*Sermon 137, 2*

PRAYER. *Listen to your King saying: "You wish to come to Me, but your grievous burdens hold you fast. Come to Me. I offer pardon for past sins; I will take the heavy burden from your shoulders."* —*Sermon 164, 4*

OCTOBER 30
He Will Be Exalted

OU mustn't think that the one who humbles himself remains lying there always since it is stated that "he will be exalted." And you mustn't suppose that this exaltation of his will occur in the sight of human beings by means of any terrestrial promotions or elevations.

You see, after saying "Blessed is the one whose upholding is from You, Lord," he went on to tie the thing up and show the spiritual loftiness of his being taken up. —*Sermon 351, 1*

PRAYER. *How hidden You are, dwelling on high in Your silence, great and only God.*

—*Confessions I, 18, 29*

160

OCTOBER 31
How Shall We Love When We See?

OVE expressed in desire is one thing; love satisfied by sight is another. I mean, you love both when you desire and when you see. For your love when you desire is aimed at arriving; your love when you see is aimed at staying.

Now if the desire of the Saints burns so hot when fueled by faith, what will it be like when fed by sight? If we love like this while we believe what we cannot yet see, how shall we love when we actually do see? —*Sermon 359A, 2*

PRAYER. *Why, Lord, having filled us with the desire to see You, by Your grace, do You hide Yourself from our eyes? For I shall never be wholly satisfied until I see You face to face.*

—*Soliloquies I, 6*

NOVEMBER 1
The Praise of Heaven

UR whole activity in heaven will consist of Amen and Alleluia. It isn't in fleeting sounds that we shall be saying Amen and Alleluia, but with the affection of mind and heart.

After all, what does Amen mean, and what is Alleluia? Amen: "It is true"; Alleluia: "Praise God." —*Sermon 362, 29*

PRAYER. *Praise be to You, glory be to You, O Fount of all mercy!* —*Confessions VI, 16, 26*

NOVEMBER 2
How To See the Raising of the Dead

ALL of us have eyes with which we can see the dead rise in the way the son of the widow rose. Not all, however, have the wherewithal to see those who are dead in the heart rise again.

To see that, you need to have already risen in the heart yourself. There is more to raising up someone to live forever than to raising up someone who will only die again. —*Sermon 98, 1*

PRAYER. *Help me, O my Strength, by which alone I can rise; help me, O infinite Virtue, which alone can sustain me; come to me, O Light, which alone is able to heal me of my interior blindness.* —*Soliloquies II, 10*

NOVEMBER 3
Does God Keep Nothing Special for the Good?

BENEFITS from the sky, benefits from the earth; the springs bubble up, the fields are fertile, the trees are laden with fruit. The good enjoy these things; the bad enjoy them too. The grateful enjoy them; the ungrateful enjoy them.

If God bestows such blessings on good and bad alike, do you suppose He keeps nothing special for the good? —*Sermon 317, 1*

PRAYER. *Let us now return to You, O Lord, that we be not overturned. Unspoilt, our good abides with You, for You are Yourself our good.* —*Confessions IV, 16, 31*

NOVEMBER 4
The Soul's Chains

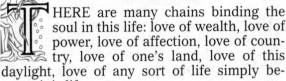HERE are many chains binding the soul in this life: love of wealth, love of power, love of affection, love of country, love of one's land, love of this daylight, love of any sort of life simply because it is life.

So while it is being held down by these chains, there comes the acid test: that if it confesses Christ, then they will all be snapped. —*Sermon 335E, 3*

PRAYER. *You, Lord, the Doer of all things, command me to praise You in them, and to confess to You and sing to Your Name.*

—*Confessions I, 7, 12*

NOVEMBER 5
Engendering Life

FATHER God and Mother Church do not engender for death as their end. They engender for eternal life because they themselves are eternal.

And we have eternal life as the inheritance promised us by Christ. —*Sermon 22, 10*

PRAYER. *May my prayer come to Your ears; my prayer wrung from me, almost extorted from me, because of my yearning for Your eternal blessings, my God!* —*On Ps. 53*

NOVEMBER 6

Tears Should Be Quickly Dried
by the Joy of Faith

IT is perfectly in order for loving hearts to grieve at the death of their dear ones, but with a sorrow that will let itself be assuaged; and to shed the tears that suit our mortal condition, but that are also prepared to be consoled.

These should be quickly dried by the joy of the faith with which we believe that when the faithful die, they depart from us only a little while, and pass on to better things. —*Sermon 172, 3*

PRAYER. *You have made us for Yourself, O Lord, and our hearts are restless until they rest in You.* —*Confessions I, 1, 1*

NOVEMBER 7

Hope in God and Have No Fear

CLING to the God by Whom you were made. Cling to Him; rely on Him; call upon Him; let Him be your strength. Say to Him: "In You, Lord, is my strength."

And in response to human threats you will sing; and the Lord Himself tells you what you must sing at the end of it all: "In God will I hope; I will not fear what mere mortal may do to me." —*Sermon 97, 4*

PRAYER. *Hearken and have mercy, my Lord and God; O Light of the blind and Strength of the weak, hearken to my soul, hear me as I cry from the depths.* —*Confessions XI, 2, 3*

NOVEMBER 8
Let Christians Be Preceded by Their Hearts

I F Christians want to practice what they know perfectly well they have openly professed, and if any of you really want to lift up your hearts, then it's up there, up there that you must deposit what you love.

Placed on earth in the flesh yourselves, live with Christ in your hearts. And just as the Church has been preceded into heaven by its Head, so let Christians be preceded by their hearts. *—Sermon 86, 1*

PRAYER. *Let us pray with all our hearts that we may live the kind of life to qualify us for a share in the heavenly kingdom.* *—Sermon 56*

NOVEMBER 9
Put Forth the Gospel

P UT forth the Gospel; with your mouth scatter the seeds you have conceived in your heart.

Let the nations hear, let the nations believe, let the nations burgeon with luxuriant growth, let a bride be born in the purple to the Lord. *—Sermon 116, 7*

PRAYER. *When we had no being, You were our refuge so that we might be born. When we were evil, You were our refuge so that we might be born anew. You are a refuge for the sustaining of those who have forsaken You.*

—Sermon on the Mount 55, 6

NOVEMBER 10
Now Is the Time of Mercy

DESPISE the time of mercy, and the time of judgment will come. Because you have been singing to me in church: "Mercy and judgment I will sing to You, O Lord." Now is the time of mercy, the time to correct ourselves; the time of judgment has not yet come. There is space; there is room. We have sinned; let us correct ourselves.

The journey is not yet over, the day has not yet drawn to a close, we have not yet breathed our last. There is no need to despair.—*Sermon 17, 5*

PRAYER. *You pluck me free, O Lord, because my eyes are fixed on Your mercy. I am miserably caught, but You mercifully extricate me.*
—*Confessions X, 34, 53*

NOVEMBER 11
Christ the Head and the Body

SINCE He is the Head of the Church, and the Church is His Body, the whole Christ is both Head and Body. He has already risen again. So we have our Head in heaven.

Our Head is interceding for us; our Head, sinless and deathless, is already placating God for our sins so that we, too, when we rise again at the end and are changed into heavenly glory, may follow our Head. —*Sermon 137, 1*

PRAYER. *Rightly is there solid hope for me in Him Who sits at Your right hand, my God, and intercedes for us.* —*Confessions X, 43, 69*

166

NOVEMBER 12
Who We Really Are

L ET us choose every day to know who we really are in case, while we are without a care in the world, the day arrives at last and, of that which we thought we were, nothing is found to be real and it is said with reference to us: "In hell who will confess to You?"

So let us work hard every day at making progress toward God. —*Sermon 16A, 13*

PRAYER. *Come, Lord, arouse us and call us back, kindle us and seize us, prove to us how sweet You are; let us love You and run to You.*
—*Confessions VIII, 4, 9*

NOVEMBER 13
Victorious with Christ

R EMEMBER, you have a commander Who has already preceded you into heaven. He has given you a way to follow, so stick to Him. Whenever you win, don't be proud and attribute it to yourself as though you had employed your own strength in the struggle.

Rather, trust in Him Who gave you the strength to win because He Himself won the victory over the world. —*Sermon 4, 37*

PRAYER. *Rejoice, says the Lord, that I am one with you, and acknowledge that you are one with Me. Behold Me as your refuge and strength.* —*Sermon 5*

NOVEMBER 14
God Is Not Displeased with
What He Has Made

GOD was displeased with our lives, and He was displeased with everything we were making of ourselves, but He was not displeased with what He had made in us.

So He will condemn what we have made, and what He has made He will save. He will condemn our evil deeds and save us in ourselves.
—*Sermon 23A, 1*

PRAYER. *Let everyone who has the aptitude listen to Your word within. How magnificent are Your works, O Lord! In wisdom You have created all things.* —*Confessions XI, 9, 11*

NOVEMBER 15
The Shortness of Life

THE whole human life is short. From infancy to decrepit old age, the whole of it is short. If Adam were still alive and then died today, what use would such length of life be to him?

It comes to this: that the very day is uncertain.
—*Sermon 17, 7*

PRAYER. *Let the soul that wanders from You understand whether it yet thirsts for You, whether yet its tears have become its daily bread; whether yet it has but one plea to make to You, that it may dwell in Your house all the days of its life.* —*Confessions XII, 11, 13*

NOVEMBER 16
Hold On to the Promises

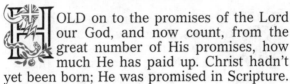OLD on to the promises of the Lord our God, and now count, from the great number of His promises, how much He has paid up. Christ hadn't yet been born; He was promised in Scripture. He paid up; He was born.

He hadn't yet suffered; He hadn't yet risen again; this too He paid up; He suffered, was crucified, and rose again. His Passion is our premium; His Blood is our redemption.

—Sermon 113A, 9

PRAYER. *These are Your promises, Lord, and who need fear to be deceived by the promises of Truth Himself?* —*Confessions XII, 1, 1*

NOVEMBER 17
God Loves To Save

HE reason why many things are kept for judgment while some things are judged here and now is in order that those whose cases are deferred may fear and be converted.

For God loves saving, not condemning, and therefore He is patient with bad people in order to make them good. —*Sermon 18, 2*

PRAYER. *Do not forsake me when I call to You since it was by Your prevenient aid that I called to You, and You have insistently pressed me to hear You from far away and be converted and begin to call to You Who were calling me.*

—Confessions XIII, 1, 1

NOVEMBER 18
Hold on to Loving Kindness

OU who are poor, hold on to loving kindness if you want to arrive, if you really want to know that what the Lord chose is loving kindness and that it's not riches as such that He condemned.

Read what Abraham was, and you will find that he was rich. The rich man went ahead and prepared hospitality for the poor. And that's just what you find in the psalm: "all together, rich and poor." —*Sermon 20A, 9*

PRAYER. *You, Lord, have made me dwell in hope, for You are unchangeable, and in You is found the rest that is mindful no more of its labors.* —*Confessions IX, 4, 11*

NOVEMBER 19
Be a Lover of a Good Life

NY of you who is a lover of a long life, be a lover of a good life instead. If you wish to live badly, a long life won't be a true good but a long evil.

So why don't you love your life enough to want it to be a good one, seeing that, even when it is bad, you prefer it to all your possessions? —*Sermon 16, 2*

PRAYER. *Give us Your everlasting blessings, Lord, but give us also the things we need in this temporal life. You have promised us the kingdom of heaven. Do not refuse us Your help in our earthly necessities.* —*Sermon 56*

NOVEMBER 20
Christ Knows How To Restore to Life

HE dead are buried deep, but Christ is high up. He knows how to heave aside the huge loads of earth with a shout.

He knows how to restore inwardly to life through His own presence, how to hand over to His disciples for unbinding. Let such people repent, then. —*Sermon 98, 7*

PRAYER. How high You are in the heights of heaven, how deep in the depths! From no place are You absent, yet how tardily do we return to You! —*Confessions VIII, 3, 8*

NOVEMBER 21
Only Charity Matters

UR Lord Jesus Christ did not choose, when telling us in advance about His judgment to come, to warn us about anything except acts of charity.

Do you imagine those on the right are not to be told: "Because you have lived chastely, because you haven't grabbed other people's property, because you have confessed faith in Me to the extent of shedding your blood"? All these good deeds, after all, must necessarily be honored in the judgment of Jesus Christ.

—*Sermon 388, 1*

PRAYER. Let our hearts go up with Jesus to heaven through the faith, hope, and charity that unite us with Him. —*Sermon on the Ascension*

NOVEMBER 22
God Is Pleased To Come

GOD isn't too grand to come; He isn't too fussy or shy; He isn't too proud. On the contrary He is pleased to come if you don't displease Him.

Listen to the promise He makes, listen to Him indeed promising with pleasure, not threatening with displeasure: "We shall come to him, I and the Father." —*Sermon 23, 6*

PRAYER. *In prayer we are asking that God's kingdom should come in us, that He may reign supreme in our hearts, and that we may be admitted to His heavenly kingdom.*

—*Sermons 56; 59*

NOVEMBER 23
Hear It Foretold, See It Fulfilled

ONCE upon a time the Christian people were not spread throughout the world. You could read about it in prophecy, but not see it on earth. Now you can both read about it and see it.

The Church itself was addressed in this sense. It wasn't told, "See, daughter, and hear," but: "Hear and see"; hear it foretold, see it fulfilled. —*Sermon 110, 4*

PRAYER. *Lead us, O Lord, to the end that will bring us perfect fulfillment and the true satisfaction of our desires. For when God is all in all, no desire will be left unfulfilled.*

—*On St. John's Gospel, Hom. 6*

NOVEMBER 24
His Praise Is Always in Our Mouths

 INCE we have all good things from God, in all our good works, when we think about the Giver of all good things, we praise God without ceasing. But when, if we lead good lives, we praise God without ceasing, we are blessing the Lord at all times, and His praise is thereby always in our mouths. —*Sermon 114A, 12*

PRAYER. *Let us praise the Lord with the whole of ourselves, not only with tongue and voice but with conscience and life and deeds.*
—*On Ps. 148, 2*

NOVEMBER 25
The Burden of Riches

 ONSIDER whether riches aren't a greater burden than poverty for you. You don't have poverty as a burden, but you do have riches as a burden. A poor man has one burden, you another.

Carry his with him, and let him carry yours with you, so that you end up by carrying your burdens for each other. —*Sermon 164, 9*

PRAYER. *"Approach Me by faith, and you will cleave to Me and I will relieve you of all your burdens so that you may be entirely Mine,"* says our Lord. —*On Ps. 33, 9*

NOVEMBER 26
Love, and You Have God

YOU don't see God. Love, and you have Him. How many things are loved in our reprehensible desires and are not had! They are greedily sought but are not, for all that, immediately possessed. —*Sermon 34, 5*

PRAYER. God is crying out to us: Love Me, and you will possess Me because you cannot love Me unless you possess Me. —*Sermon 34*

NOVEMBER 27
God's Healing Surgery

THE doctor sometimes makes a mistake, but God never does. So if you entrust yourself to a doctor who can sometimes make mistakes, you are entrusting yourself to human treatment. And won't you allow God to cut, to slice off some of your profits if, by such a check, you may have a lesson to learn?

So then, brothers and sisters, be upright of heart; that is, do not get annoyed with God for any reason at all. —*Sermon 15A, 8-9*

PRAYER. O my inward Healer, let my heart keep watch for Your loving mercy and Your gentle grace, through which every weak soul that knows its own weakness grows strong.
—*Confessions X, 3, 4*

NOVEMBER 28
When You Arrive, You Will Enjoy God

A S a traveler, you are walking by faith and by hope. When you arrive, you will enjoy Him Whom you have loved as you traveled on your journey.

It is He Who founded the native country to which you should be hastening to come. He has sent you a letter from there that you are not to put off your return from your travels.

—*Sermon 22A, 4*

PRAYER. *O wondrous home! O land where there is no anxiety; where there are no enemies, no injury; where we shall live in safety and never wish to depart since no safer place is to be found.* —*Sermon 217*

NOVEMBER 29
Fruitful Sorrow

W E have no grounds for finding fault with God. There will be nothing for us to say against Him when He comes to judge.

Let us all think about our own sins and amend them now while there is still time. Let us have fruitful sorrow, not sterile repentance.

—*Sermon 22, 6*

PRAYER. *You, Lord, abide forever and will not forever be angry with us, for You have taken pity on us who are earth and ashes.*

—*Confessions VII, 8, 12*

NOVEMBER 30
Pray for the Fulfillment of Justice

WE should not be praying for worldly things that come and go and vanish like the smoke.

What we should be praying for is the fulfillment of justice and the hallowing of God's Name, not for getting the better of the lust and the greed inside; not for the feeling of the flesh, but for the taming of avarice. That's what our prayers should be about: helping us in our inner struggles till they crown us in our final victory. —*Sermon 40, 7*

PRAYER. *Let us persevere in longing until the promise comes true and sighing is a thing of the past and unalloyed rejoicing takes its place.* —*On Ps. 148, 1*

DECEMBER 1
Think About How Much Ground
Has Still To Be Traveled

WHAT you ought to do is not to think about how much ground you have covered.

Rather, think about how much you still have left until you finish the journey and can enjoy yourself in your home country, being lifted up by the king of that country Who, for your sake, humbled Himself. —*Sermon 16B, 3*

PRAYER. *Take possession of My very self, says the Lord. Enjoy Me, embrace Me. You are not yet wholly equal to it; lay hold of Me by faith, and you shall cleave to Me.* —*On Ps. 33, 2*

DECEMBER 2
The Inheritance

THE whole Body has not received the inheritance because the Head is in heaven, the members still on earth. Nor is the Head going to receive the inheritance alone, leaving the Body behind.

The whole Christ is going to receive the inheritance, the whole Man, that is to say, Head and Body. —*Sermon 22, 10*

PRAYER. *Christ's possession and heritage and Body, the one Church, this unity which is ourselves, cries out from the ends of the earth: "Hear my cry, O God; listen to my prayer. From the ends of the earth I cry out to You."*
—*On Ps. 60*

DECEMBER 3
Do Not Come Fruitlessly to Church

I WISH to warn you, dearly beloved, not to come fruitlessly to church by hearing so many good things and yet not acting well. Instead, following the goodness of the sower and the seed, which is the word of God, let a wonderfully abundant crop of good works spring up in your characters and in your lives as in a good soil. —*Sermon 23A, 1*

PRAYER. *O Christ, You Who are sitting at the right hand of the Father and yet labor on earth in Your feet and members: to us You say, "What is your hope?"* —*Sermon 9*

DECEMBER 4
Restraint and Endurance

 UST as it is the task of restraint not to trust in the well-being of the world, so it is the task of endurance not to succumb to the ill-being of the world.

So whether we have never had it so good or whether we have never had it so bad, we must wait for the Lord, wait for Him to give us what is truly good and pleasant, and ward off from us what is truly evil. —*Sermon 38, 1*

PRAYER. *O Strength of my soul, make Your way in and shape it to Yourself, that it may be Yours to have and to hold, free from stain or wrinkle.* —*Confessions X, 1, 1*

DECEMBER 5
What Was Promised Has Been Fulfilled

EALIZE that the One Who made you the promises is truthful and trustworthy. He hasn't yet shown you everything because it isn't yet time for Him to do so.

But He has already shown you a great many things. What was promised has been fulfilled; what was foretold has been fulfilled. —*Sermon 38, 10*

PRAYER. *There is but one hope, one reliance, one solid promise, O God, and that is Your mercy.* —*Confessions X, 32, 48*

DECEMBER 6
What Jesus Wills Is Not Unfair

JESUS came as a little one to little ones, He came as a doctor to the sick, He that could come when He would, go back when He would: that's justice.

That which He wills, surely, is not unfair, nor can that be fair which He does not will.

—Sermon 126, 4

PRAYER. *Rescue me, Lord, in the justice that is Yours: the justice that makes the ungodly godly, the unrighteous righteous, the blind to see clearly, the falling to stand on their feet, and mourners to go on their way rejoicing.*

—On Ps. 30, 2

DECEMBER 7
In Christ the Promises Are True

WALK along the narrow but sure way that leads to the wide open spaces of the heavenly Jerusalem, which is our eternal mother.

Hope with unshakable conviction for what you cannot yet see; wait patiently for what you do not yet possess; because you can be assured with absolute confidence that in Christ you have One Whose promises are true. *—Sermon 157, 6*

PRAYER. *Allow me, Lord, to seek still further; O my Hope, do not let my intentions fail.*

—Confessions XI, 18, 23

DECEMBER 8

It Means More that Mary Was
a Disciple of Christ

IDN'T the Virgin Mary do the will of the Father? I mean, she believed by faith, she conceived by faith, she was chosen to be the one from whom Salvation in the very midst of the human race would be born for us, she was created by Christ before Christ was created in her. Holy Mary did the will of the Father.

And therefore it means more for Mary to have been a disciple of Christ than to have been Christ's Mother. —*Sermon 72A, 7*

PRAYER. *What are you who are to become a mother? How have you deserved and obtained this gift? How comes this immense good to you? He Who made you is made in you. He is made in you by Whom you came to be.* —*Sermon 291, 5*

DECEMBER 9

Wait for the Lord

HAT does "Wait for the Lord" mean? Receive only when He gives; don't demand whenever you want.

It's not yet the time for giving. He has waited for you; now you wait for Him.

—*Sermon 40, 1*

PRAYER. *O Lord, have mercy on me and grant what I desire.* —*Confessions XI, 2, 4*

DECEMBER 10
The Catholic Faith

IF our Lord Jesus Christ had not been prepared to become human, humanity would have perished. He became what He had made, that what He had made might not perish.

True Man, true God; God and Man, the whole Christ. This is the Catholic faith.

—Sermon 92, 3

PRAYER. *In my Lord, the Son of Man, Your right hand upholds me that I may be set free from what I once was and follow after Your Oneness.* *—Confessions XI, 29, 39*

DECEMBER 11
Love Is the Root of All Good Things

BECAUSE Jesus has brought the newness of life into action against the oldness of death, He Himself sets a new commandment against the old sin.

Any of you, then, who wish to extinguish the old sin, douse cupidity with the new commandment and embrace love. Just as cupidity, you see, is the root of all evils, so is love the root of all good things. *—Sermon 350, 1*

PRAYER. *You shed light on me and give me joy, O God, You offer Yourself, lovable and longed for, that I may thrust myself away in disgust and choose You, and be pleasing no more either to You or to myself except in what I have from You.* *—Confessions X, 2, 2*

DECEMBER 12
Choices

WHAT we get afterward we choose here; and what we reap there we sow here.

That's why as long as we live we should be on the watch and should be choosing what we are going to keep in the future.

—Sermon 97, 3

PRAYER. *My God, preserve Your gifts in me. So will You preserve me too, and what You have given me will grow and reach perfection, and I will be with You; for my existence itself is Your gift.* *—Confessions I, 20, 31*

DECEMBER 13
Let Others Cross Over Too

ARE you demanding God's severity? Since you have crossed over yourself, let others cross over too. It isn't the case that because you have already crossed over you have cut the bridge of God's mercy behind you. There are still others to cross over.

He made you good when you were bad; He wants the same for others, to become good from being bad, just as you, from being bad, were made good. *—Sermon 113A, 12*

PRAYER. *Look down in mercy, Lord, and set us free who already call upon You. Set free those also who do not yet call upon You, so that they may invoke You and You may give them freedom.* *—Confessions I, 10, 16*

DECEMBER 14

If You Want To Get to These Things
Don't Disdain Those

HOEVER boasts "should boast in the Lord." Christ crucified! Where there's humility, there's majesty; where there's weakness, there's might; where there's death, there's life.

If you want to get to these things, don't disdain those. —*Sermon 160, 4*

PRAYER. *You have loved me more than Your own self, Lord, since our life has been dearer to You than Your own and it was Your will to die in order to preserve us from death.*

—*Soliloquies XIII, 4*

DECEMBER 15

Moving Along

F we are all moving along, let us perform some work which cannot move on, so that, when we have moved on and come to where we shall no longer move again, we may find our good works waiting for us there.

Christ the Lord is their keeper. Why are you afraid of losing what you invest with generosity? —*Sermon 111, 4*

PRAYER. *Perfect Your work in me, O Lord. Your voice is joy to me, ringing out above a flood of joys.* —*Confessions XI, 2, 3*

DECEMBER 16
The Marvel of God's Word

HERE I am making a word for you, and you all have it. It's not just that you all have it, but that you all have it all. It has reached you all; it has all reached every one of you.

Isn't my word marvelous! So what must the Word of God be?
—Sermon 120, 3

PRAYER. *You, Lord, are evidently inviting us to understand that the word in question is that Word Who is God, God with You Who are God; He is uttered eternally, and through Him are eternally uttered all things.*

—Confessions XI, 7, 9

DECEMBER 17
Christ Our Home and Our Way

CHRIST as God is the home country we are going to; Christ as Man is the way we are going by. It's to Him we are going, by Him we are going; why are we afraid of going wrong?

So now, having already suffered through that humility, already died, already been buried, already risen and ascended into heaven, He is both there, seated at the right hand of the Father, and here, suffering want in His poor.
—Sermon 123, 3

PRAYER. *O happy home! O land of safety! May I dwell there in security!* *—Sermon 217, 2*

DECEMBER 18
What Must the Creator Be?

I HAVE been speaking; what I have said has gone out to you, and hasn't departed from me. It has reached you, and has not been separated from me.

I am a creature, you are creatures; and so many wonderful things occur with my word, in my thoughts, in my mouth, in my voice, in your ears, in your thoughts. What must the Creator be? —*Sermon 120, 3*

PRAYER. It was You, O Lord, Who created the heavens and earth. They are beautiful because You are beautiful. They are good because You are good. They have come to be because You are. —*Confessions XI, 4, 5*

DECEMBER 19
A Marvelous Exchange

F OR your sakes the Word "became flesh." For your sakes the One Who was the Son of God became the Son of Man, in order that you who were sons of men might be turned into sons of God.

He was the Son of God and He became the Son of Man. You were sons of men and you have become sons of God. He has shared with us our ills, and He is going to give us His goods. —*Sermon 121, 5*

PRAYER. Glory to our Lord. The Truth, clad in flesh, came and healed through His flesh the inner eye of our heart, that afterward we might be able to see Him face to face. —*On Ps. 56, 17*

DECEMBER 20

The Word Took Up Our Grass in Order
To Make Us into Gold

THE Word of God took up our grass in order to make us into gold. The Lord suffered for us, was buried, rose again, ascended into heaven, and is seated at the Father's right hand, no longer grass but now gold, undestroyed and indestructible.

So we are promised a change, a transmutation, and yet while we are approaching that transmutation, we will be passing through this grass phase. —*Sermon 113B, 2*

PRAYER. *O Lord, give us Your Christ; let us know and see Him—and rejoice.* —*On Ps. 84, 9*

DECEMBER 21

He Came to the Captives Who
Knew No Captivity

IF we hadn't been held in captivity, we wouldn't have needed a redeemer. So He came to the captives not having been captured Himself. He came to redeem the captives having in Himself no trace of captivity, that is to say of iniquity, but bringing the price for us in His mortal flesh.

You see, if He hadn't had mortal flesh, where would the Word have found blood to shed for the captives? —*Sermon 27, 2*

PRAYER. *How You loved us, O good Father, Who spared not even Your only Son, but gave Him up for us evildoers!* —*Confessions X, 43, 69*

DECEMBER 22
Christ Is Born!

CHRIST is born; God from the Father, Man from His Mother; from the Father's immortality, from the Mother's virginity; from the Father without mother, from His Mother without father; from the Father timelessly, from His Mother seedlessly; from the Father as the beginning of life, from His Mother as the end of death; from the Father to regulate every day, from His Mother to consecrate this day. —*Sermon 194, 1*

PRAYER. *O Loveliness that does not deceive, Loveliness happy and abiding!* —*Confessions II, 1, 1*

DECEMBER 23
How Did Christ Become Flesh and Not Depart from the Father?

WE wonder how Christ could take flesh, be born of a virgin and not depart from the Father. But look, here am I now speaking to you; before this I was thinking about what I was going to say to you, and there was already a word in my mind. I mean, I wouldn't be saying it to you unless I had thought of it first.

Just as my word assumed sound in order to be heard, so the Word of God assumed flesh in order to be seen. —*Sermon 225, 3*

PRAYER. *Open my inward ears with the power of Your word so that I may hear Your oracles of wisdom. They will hear Your voice when You employ the power of Your word.* —*Soliloquies I, 2*

DECEMBER 24
Christ Stooped Down To Raise Us Up

WHEN you hear that "Truth has sprung from the earth," it is stating Christ's condescension, not His condition; His kindness not His wretchedness.

In order that Truth might spring from the earth, He came down from heaven. In order that the Bridegroom might come forth from His chamber, His going forth was from the height of heaven. That is why He was born today. —*Sermon 192, 3*

PRAYER. *O eternal Truth, true Love, and beloved Eternity, You are my God, and for You I sigh day and night.* —*Confessions VII, 10, 16*

DECEMBER 25
Let Us Give Birth to Praise

LET Christ's mercy come to be in our hearts. His Mother bore Him in her womb; let us bear Him in our hearts. The Virgin was big with the incarnation of Christ; let our bosoms grow big with the faith of Christ. She gave birth to the Savior; let us give birth to praise.

We mustn't be barren; our souls must be fruitful with God. —*Sermon 189, 3*

PRAYER. *Lord, You cried to me from afar: "I am Who am." I heard it as one hears a word in the heart.* —*Confessions VII, 10, 16*

DECEMBER 26
I See the Heavens Opened

STEPHEN could see Jesus standing. The reason He was standing and not sitting is that, standing up above and watching from above His soldier battling down below, He was supplying him with invincible strength so that he shouldn't fall.

"Behold," Stephen said, "I see the heavens opened." Blessed indeed the man to whom the heavens lie open! —*Sermon 314, 1*

PRAYER. *O God, before You stand my strength and my weakness; preserve the one and heal the other, I pray.* —*On the Trinity XV, 51*

DECEMBER 27
The Word Was Hidden with the Father

IF we may be permitted to compare tiny things with great ones, the lowest with the highest, the human with the Divine, God has done that too.

The Word was hidden with the Father. In order to come to us, He commandeered a kind of vehicle; He took flesh to Himself. He came forth to us and did not depart from the Father.

—*Sermon 223A, 2*

PRAYER. *O invisible Light of truth and wisdom that all the light of sun or of eyes could never bring to light: bathe my soul in the blessed and holy depths of Your light so that wherever it may be it may see You in Yourself and contemplate itself in You.* —*Soliloquies XIII, 1*

189

DECEMBER 28
God Became a Human Being

GOD became a Human Being, so that in one Person you could have both something to see and something to believe. "In the beginning was the Word, and the Word was with God, and the Word was God." You hear, and you don't yet see. Lo and behold He comes; lo and behold, He's born.

Here in the very moment of birth, here already there are two things, both One you can see and One you can't. But this is so that by the One you can see you may believe in the One you can't see. —*Sermon 126, 5*

PRAYER. *O Word by Whom time was made, born in time although You are eternal life, You call us who are bound by time and make us eternal.* —*On Ps. 101, 10*

DECEMBER 29
Christ Our Way and Destination

BY Christ as Man, you wend your way to Christ as God. God is too much for you, but God became Man. What was a long way away from you has come down right next to you through a Man.

The place for you to stay in, that's God; the way for you to get there, that's Man. It's one and the same Christ, both the Way to go by and the Place to go to. —*Sermon 261,7*

PRAYER. *O Word of God, bring me into that transport of delight from which Divine joys flow.* —*Soliloquies I, 8*

DECEMBER 30

The Wonder That One Who Was Born in This Way Was Willing To Be Born at All

THE power is certainly wonderful, but still more to be wondered at is the loving kindness: that the One Who was able to be born in this way was willing to be born at all!

He was already the only Son of the Father when He was born as the only Son of His Mother. And He that was made in His Mother had already made His Mother for Himself.

—*Sermon 192, 1*

PRAYER. *Open my heart by the outpouring of Your wisdom and enlighten it with one ray of that wisdom so that it may meditate on all the things You have done for it.* —*Soliloquies VII, 2*

DECEMBER 31

Let Us Remain in His Word

WE who believe in Christ, let us remain in His word. Because if we remain in His word, we are truly His disciples.

Not only the Twelve but all of us who remain in His word, are truly His disciples. We will know the Truth, and the Truth will deliver us, i.e., Christ, the Son of God. —*Sermon 134, 6*

PRAYER. *O supreme Truth, O true and infinite Greatness, You have made us sharers in Your glory and bestowed on us the capacity of becoming Your children, conformed to the likeness of Your glorious Son.* —*Soliloquies VIII, 4*

PRAYER

Breathe into me, Holy Spirit,
that my thoughts may all be holy.
Move in me, Holy Spirit,
that my work, too, may be holy.
Attract my heart, Holy Spirit,
that I may love only what is holy.
Strengthen me, Holy Spirit,
that I may defend all that is holy.
Protect me, Holy Spirit,
that I always may be holy.

Attributed to St. Augustine

OTHER OUTSTANDING CATHOLIC BOOKS

AUGUSTINE ON PRAYER—An excellent summary of the great African Bishop's teaching on prayer in the life of Christians. Over 500 Augustinian texts. **Ask for No. 171**

SAINT AUGUSTINE: Man, Pastor, Mystic—By Rev. Augustine Trapé, O.S.A. A masterful biography of one of the greatest Saints in the Church by a world-renowned scholar. Large type and magnificently illustrated. **Ask for No. 172**

CONFESSIONS OF ST. AUGUSTINE—New translation of the Christian classic that—after the Bible and the Imitation of Christ—is the most widely translated and the most universally esteemed. It is published in prayerbook format as befits its nature.. **Ask for No. 173**

WORDS OF COMFORT FOR EVERY DAY—Short meditation for every day including a Scripture text and a meditative prayer to God the Father. Printed in two colors. 192 pages. **Ask for No. 186**

MARY DAY BY DAY—Minute meditations for every day of the year, including a Scripture passage, a quotation from the Saints, and a concluding prayer. Printed in two colors with over 300 illustrations. **Ask for No. 180**

MINUTE MEDITATIONS FROM THE POPES—By Rev. Jude Winkler, O.F.M. Conv. Minute meditations for every day of the year using the words of twentieth-century Popes. Printed and illustrated in two colors. **Ask for No. 175**

BIBLE DAY BY DAY—By Rev. John Kersten, S.V.D. Minute Bible meditations for every day including a short Scripture text and brief reflection. Printed in two colors with 300 illustrations. **Ask for No. 150**

LIVING WISDOM FOR EVERY DAY—By Rev. Bennet Kelley, C.P. Choice texts from St. Paul of the Cross, one of the true Masters of Spirituality, and a prayer for each day. **Ask for No. 182**

MINUTE MEDITATIONS FOR EACH DAY— By Rev. Bede Naegele O.C.D. This very attractive book offers a short Scripture text, a practical reflection, and a meaningful prayer for each day of the year. **Ask for No. 190**

WHEREVER CATHOLIC BOOKS ARE SOLD